THE SINGING HEART OF THE WORLD

John Feehan

The Singing Heart of the World
CREATION, EVOLUTION AND FAITH

the columba press

First published in 2010 by
the columba press
55A Spruce Avenue, Stillorgan Industrial Park, Blackrock, Co Dublin

Cover by Bill Bolger
Cover picture by Brigid Birney
Origination by The Columba Press
Printed in Ireland by ColourBooks Ltd, Dublin

ISBN 1-85607-677-7

Table of Contents

Preface

On the edge of one of the many islands at the southern end of Lough Oughter stands the Abbey of the Holy Trinity. This is where the bishops of Armagh Archdiocese met in 1651 in the aftermath of Cromwell's campaign in Ireland. Here too, the *Annals of Lough Cé* were compiled in 1588 so that the storied past of the island might not be altogether lost in the new dispensation that was fast approaching.

Trinity Island priory had been founded in 1237, the year in which Thomas Aquinas celebrated his 12th birthday. For over three centuries the monks of this isolated and beautiful place served their community, secure in the theological framework of the newly-minted Thomist certainty that explained the meaning and direction of their world insofar as human understanding had yet apprehended it. This oasis of endeavour stood like a beacon that enshrined the possibility of a better way of life and the hope of a richer future, before the splendid doorway that welcomed visitors under its roof was dismantled and taken away, and its walls crumbled and fell.

Warm and secure inside its insulated walls, I write these opening words in Trinity Lodge, overlooking the ruined abbey as the winds of January sweep over the lake. I try to imagine the world of the forgotten scribe who formed his letters with frozen fingers down there on the lake's edge more than four centuries ago. A future more different than he could have imagined lay around the very next corner of his time. Cocooned here in the isolated comfort of Trinity Lodge, it is hard to believe that beyond this wooded island we face into a future that will see change on an unprecedented scale that dwarfs the change that saw the demise of the Abbey of the Holy Trinity: a future in which the framework of faith is being shaken by a way of being-in-the-world that is not unduly concerned with the notion of God or godly behaviour. And yet the only future that can command our allegiance is one in which concern for reason and virtue, as the only secure foundation and direction for human behaviour, is championed.

What will Trinity Island be like four centuries hence? Four hundred years from now the oaks will have grown to full stature, our fate over that time remembered in the growth rings of its future. Each of us must shed what little light we can within the circle of our limited influence. We must hope that the reinforcing aureoles of the light from each of us will provide enough illumination for the short leg of the great journey in which it is given us to carry the lamp. And so, I put to paper thoughts that have preoccupied me for several decades, and began to crystallise into words in more recent years through my involvement with the Ecology and Religion Programme of the Columbans at Dalgan Park. My hope and faith is that under the mature oaks of Trinity Island in 300 years, the O'Dowds (a tribe in these parts) will still keep the faith, however many moults that faith may have undergone in the meantime in its unceasing metamorphosis.

Trinity Island Lodge
January 2009

Foreword

I had a privileged childhood, growing up close to nature, born with the sound of a river in my ears, with meadows at my doorstep in which corncrakes nested, and the untouched bog beyond where nightjars still churred on summer evenings in the 1960s. Before I was ten I had fallen in love with birds and flowers. And I had the great good fortune to encounter a teacher who encouraged my early love of botany in secondary school, in the very early years of a fifteen-year journey towards a priesthood not intended for me. Those years helped me to keep my attention on questions and concerns I might have found less time for if I had to juggle with all of the distractions and challenges most of us have to deal with at that age. They led me to Teilhard de Chardin in my late teens, and at the same time I began the study of natural science and the philosophy of Bernard Lonergan that has informed my search for meaning ever since.

The recurring theme of the book is that our beliefs, values and behaviour must be informed by reason, which is guided by the way of understanding grounded in experience that is the hallmark of modern science, which is rooted by historical accident in the 'western tradition'. However, although that mode of knowing is fundamental, it is insufficiently attentive to the 'information content' of the universe of our experience, and a deeper and closer attention is indispensable if we are to articulate a response to which we may attach the label 'religious'. The argument, therefore, is that the affirmation of faith in a supernatural 'being' we call God is more deeply reasonable and more true to what greater openness to the universe reveals than is its negation. I use the word 'supernatural' here not to mean something that is altogether beyond nature, but in the way we use it in 'supermarket' to mean something that is still a market, but much more: except that here we have no way of expressing infinite number of powers of 'super' the prefix must be raised to! More briefly I attempt to restate the argument for a 'superpersonal' God, and I review the outlines of the ethical imperative and social arrangements to which a rational faith points.

The central tenet of the book is that reason is not compromised by faith: that there is indeed a reciprocity between reason and faith: but it only comes into focus with a widening of the embrace of rationality on the part of reason: just as faith needs to embrace and fully incorporate the deeper appreciation of the creation our new understanding of cosmogenesis and evolution requires it to. Indeed, I believe that what is needed is nothing less than the metamorphosis of faith, using that word in the sense in which it is used to describe the radical transformation that takes place in the lives of higher insects: where the adult may appear totally different in form from the larval stage, yet is essentially the same, and the latter is preparation for the former. But perhaps indeed a comparable metamorphosis is required of science ...

I hope that my absolute commitment to unconditional human understanding, based on the totality of human experience, will be clear on every page of what follows. My criticism of 'science' is simply that it is not scientific enough in the sense that it does not embrace the totality of experience, only those dimensions that can be measured and quantified. On the other hand, my critique of faith is that its embrace of scientific understanding is, to varying degrees, selective.

No doubt it would take as many volumes as the *Summa Theologiae* to do justice to any of this, and I do not have the conceptual or linguistic brilliance required for this: but when all is said and done, what matters is to try to convey the notion that what and who, for want of any better word, we call God is *real*, even if the prism of our physical reality can only see the colours which the refractive medium of our human crystal allows.

Ribes sanguineum, the flowering currant,
her back to the limestone wall and
silent all winter, bursts
into song in March, all bells and cymbals,
wind chimes and tinkle triangles,
calling the early bees to feast.

I expect you think
I have mixed my metaphors again:
as if carefully sorted figures of speech
and balanced syntax could get it right,
could frame the melody the flowering currant sang
with the morning light and the March wind
and the harkening Andrena
hastening.

And now I know
the answer to what we asked
each other often is where the currant sings
and swings its bells in the morning light,
never to be contained and held
in word. It does not need our words, it will
vanish with our attempts to name
its song.
                    Which is why
poetry succeeds, looking sideways
at the singing heart of the world.

John Feehan, *By the Grace of God*, 14

For Hugh

The Nature of Science

I say, therefore, that one science is the mistress of the others, namely, theology, to which the remaining sciences are vitally necessary and without which [theology] cannot reach its end.

Francis Bacon, *Opus Majus,* Part 2, Chapter I

For many people science is synonymous with brainy people in white coats discovering and inventing things in laboratories with incomprehensibly complex equipment. It is the application of these discoveries through technology that underpins our modern comfortable way of life. Almost nothing we do is untouched by its all-pervading influence. On the other hand, of course, 'science' is responsible for many of the great problems and dilemmas of our age. It is technology that has given us the weaponry that makes modern warfare so devastating; on the other hand, medical technology has given us control over disease, enabling the human population to reach proportions that now threaten the life support systems of the planet with its impact. It is a scenario that many find daunting and intimidating. And when we are told that most scientists don't believe in God, it can give rise to feelings of inadequacy and insecurity in those who do profess faith.

The stupendous achievement that is modern science stands at the end of a long history.[1] The incomprehensible equipment we observe at CERN or in the laboratory has a history and can be traced back to simple beginnings that over the centuries have developed and become ever more elaborated and complex. The gargantuan enterprise that is modern science is a cumulative enterprise built over centuries, each generation building on the insight and achievement of those who have gone before. But the essential mode of enquiry that underpins the scientific endeavour has not changed in all that time. To see what this is, let us strip away the accumulated paraphernalia of the laboratory and look at an early example of science at work.

The man who measured the size of the earth with a stick:
Eratosthenes and Alexandria

The capacity to interrogate nature in this way, and come to understand how it works, is part of human intelligence, of what distinguishes us from other creatures (though in a broader sense, of course, all creatures are intelligent). It is at work in all of us. Only very recently has it crystallised out as a distinct and separate method of enquiry. A good example of the scientific mode of investigation is provided by Eratosthenes (276-194 BC), the man who measured the earth's circumference with nothing more than a ruler – and his brain. Eratosthenes lived and worked in 3rd century BC Alexandria (where he was director of the great library). He made several notable contributions in mathematics and physics (he was a close friend of the more famous Archimedes), but is best remembered for his calculation of the earth's circumference. Alexandria was the greatest city the western world had until that time ever seen, and its greatest marvel was the library there and its associated museum. It flourished for 700 years, and was the centre to which much of the genius of the age gravitated. In addition to Eratosthenes himself, there were men such as Hipparchus, Euclid, Dionysius of Thrace, Herophilus, Heron of Alexandria, Apollonius of Perga, Ptolemy and Archimedes, and at the very end the great woman mathematician and astronomer, Hypatia. The library could have contained up to half a million books, each a handwritten papyrus scroll. Only a small fraction of its titles survive.

Eratosthenes read in one of the books in his library that, at the southern frontier post of Syene, near the first cataract of the Nile and 800km south of Alexandria and situated exactly on the Tropic of Cancer, vertical columns or upright posts cast no shadow at noon on the longest day of the year: the summer solstice on 21 June. On that day the sun shone vertically down the deepest well shaft. The sun, in other words, was directly overhead. But in Alexandria on that day the sun did cast a shadow at noon. Eratosthenes reasoned that this could not happen if the earth were flat. The sun is effectively an infinite distance away, at least so far away in practice that by the time its rays reach the earth they are parallel. If the earth were flat the sun should shine directly down the wells both at Alexandria and Syene when the sun is directly overhead. When it is not directly overhead, the sun should cast shadows of equal length at both places. The only rational explanation, Eratosthenes reasoned, is that the surface of the earth is curved. Moreover, the angle the sun makes with a vertical rod at Alexandria, when it is directly overhead at Syene, must be equal to the angle an extension of that rod to the centre of the earth makes with a continuation to the centre of the earth of a vertical rod at Syene (7°). Knowing the horizontal distance between Alexandria and Syene (he hired a man to pace it out for him) only the simplest of geometry is required to determine that the circumference of the earth must be 40,000km (800km x 50 – 7° is about a fiftieth of a full circle). This is the correct answer, which the most accurate modern calculations show to be out by no more than a few percent (the modern estimate is 40,076km).

What we see here is the exercise of observation, intelligence, deduction, experiment: the things which in time come to weave the way of seeing we call *science*. Eratosthenes observed certain enigmatic features of the world in which he lived. At noon on the summer solstice a vertical pole at Syene casts a shadow but not at Alexandria. How is this to be explained? His mind then goes to work, assembling and sorting other relevant information before everything clicks into place and a hypothesis is formulated in terms of the observable already 'known' laws of nature. Because this is so, predictions can be made on the basis of the hypothesis, experiments can be devised and carried out to test them, and if it survives these it will be elevated to the status of a theory. If it fails a single test its validity is in question: it will need to be refined, and in some cases discarded.

The most important thing to notice, from our point of view, is the way Eratosthenes looks at the evidence presented to his senses, asks questions about what is going on, and uses his intelligence to arrive at an explanation that is consistent with the evidence: formulating in the process a hypothesis about how things actually work. Sometimes the tools used to facilitate that process will need to be more complicated than Eratosthenes' gnomon[2] (how long a journey lies between that and the particle accelerator at CERN!): and the hypothesis arrived at will always need to be substantiated by further experiments, carefully formulated in such as way that they will put it to the test. If it survives this process of testing, then it can be considered a theory of how this particular aspect of reality works. That is the second key element in science: it tells us how the world actually works: it corresponds with reality, the real world. It reaches its conclusions and bases its predictions on the actual evidence before our senses, never on hearsay or speculation, presumption or tradition. Notice, too, the way mathematics is used to give measured precision to the explanation of what is going on.

There you have the scientific mode of enquiry laid bare, without its modern bells and trimmings and all the investigative paraphernalia it has acquired over the centuries. It is nothing more or less than the use of the human mind, unfettered by opinion or tradition, to uncover secret by slow secret, cumulatively over time, the workings of the world. It increases our wonder and delight at how amazing and beautiful and intelligent the world is – and the universe of which it is part. It is not primarily concerned with whether this knowledge is useful, whether we can turn our gaze inwards and ask how can we use this understanding to improve human life, my life.

Aristotle (384-322 BC)

The early progress of this mode of enquiry was very slow and – as a professional enterprise – confined to one corner of the world. It is essentially a mode of enquiry whose aim is to understand the world. As such it is something we are all capable of when we put our minds to work; and as such it has always been used by people to shape the material and cultural fabric of human society – but not in the dedicated and deliberate fashion of what is often described as the Ionian Awakening in ancient Greece.

Aristotle is generally thought of as the father of modern science. At the heart of everything his enquiring mind probed is the axiom that it is from the appearances – the evidence – that we must start in our search for knowledge.[3] In spite of his brilliance, Aristotle's achievement was limited by the fact that he was the first to look scientifically at most of the subjects he investigated. Basic concepts such as mass, velocity, temperature and force had not as yet been clarified, and it would be 1800

Aristotle, marble portrait bust, Roman copy (2nd century BC) of a Greek original (c. 325 BC); in the Museo Nazionale Romano, Rome.

years before the key notion of applying mathematics to quantify observations in physics would be developed, and the experimental apparatus needed to measure time and temperature accurately had not been invented. He also had a tendency to elevate provisional hypotheses based on the limited observations he could carry out to the status of Laws of the Universe. One such was his geocentric cosmology – the idea that the earth is at the centre of the universe – which remained the dominant view until the 16th century, when it was shown to be a wrong interpretation of limited evidence. Aristotle's logic is still, however, an essential foundation for clear thinking.

What is science?
Science, then, is the unending quest to understand the world about us, and the wider universe of which it is a tiny part. It has however come to be more particularly identified with seeking to understand how it works, and to apply that understanding for the betterment of human life. It sets out to discover what the observable world is telling us about itself. It takes the evidence that it presents to our senses, and asks: what is going on here? – and again, in the more particular sense just referred to, how is this being done: how does it work? The question is directed at one facet of reality at a time, and so the scientific enterprise is broken, like the ray of light passing through a glass prism, into a multiplicity of disciplines, each with its endless array of questions. It is also progressive: it evolves over time, the achievement of any

one generation building upon the accumulated knowledge of those who have gone before. In the beginning, the evidence is gathered directly by our senses, but our growing understanding enables us to construct extensions to our senses, so that we can see further and deeper: the most familiar such extensions being the telescope and the microscope.

The insistence on proof via experiment is one of the foundations of science: you establish a hypothesis on the basis of the information to hand, and then you devise an experiment or series of experiments to test it (which often requires great ingenuity in itself), and if it survives the test, you formulate a theory: which still leaves an open mind as to what the future may reveal.

Science has proved its ability to explain the workings of reality. What we are more concerned with here, however, are the implications for the *meaning* of reality. Science has problems with religion because of religion's insistence on revealed truth: a 'revelation' other than the creation that is. Science considers itself to be more founded, grounded, than revelation in this sense: it believes that it provides the only secure foundation for human understanding and behaviour.

The rebirth of scientific enquiry

'Science' as we define it today is a relatively recent development in human history. People have always asked questions of the world about them, but in the beginning and for a long time, although the outline of an answer was always suggested by the evidence, that outline might then be elaborated in explanations that the evidence did not support. It is worth remembering what the root of that critical word 'evidence' is: that which is before our eyes, that which our senses confront. We can perhaps trace the formal beginning of the intellectual journey that became the highway of science today in a famous statement of Aristotle: 'The faculty of thinking thinks the forms in the images' – but the images must come first.

In 415 AD the library of Alexandria was destroyed by a Christian mob with the blessing of Cyril, Archbishop of Alexandria (later Saint Cyril). With its destruction the accumulated wisdom enshrined there was virtually obliterated. Not a single scroll remains today. Hypatia herself was dragged from her chariot, stripped of her clothes and flayed alive with abalone shells in the name of Christ. Then her body was burned. What happened at Alexandria is a lesson for our times of the capacity of religion that has broken with reason to destroy our advance towards a more mature understanding of divinity and of our place in the scheme of things. In its shadow we must pause and consider before we cast the first Christian stone at contemporary and comparable Muslim fanaticism.[4]

The destruction of the Alexandrian archive smothered the small flame of scientific knowledge that had grown from the Ionian awakening, and heralded a descent into a dark age: not in the sense we usually use the term to denote the chaos that followed the collapse of the Roman Empire, but because the mode of enquiry that is science was suppressed by early Christianity. The accumulated knowledge of eight centuries was irrevocably lost, and it would be another eight centuries before the process of recovery began.

Thomas Aquinas

The rediscovery of the scientific approach owed much to the enquiries of medieval Islamic scholars who rediscovered the works of Aristotle, and it was through these intermediaries – very notable thinkers in themselves – that the thinking of Aristotle reached the Christian west. In the early 13th century Thomas Aquinas made the thinking of Aristotle his own and wove it into an intellectually mesmerising tapestry – but it was a tapestry with a woof as well as a warp: the woof of scientific knowing was crossed with the warp of revealed knowledge.[5] Scholasticism, however, froze the God-centred Aristotelianism of Thomas in its 13th century clothing; in the centuries that followed no serious attempt was made to review it in light of the advance of scientific knowledge, with the result that knots of contradiction inevitably developed, leading to the rejection of the entire tapestry by the scientific mind. Eventually in the west, science and religion went their separate ways. In Islam, where life is still seen more as all of a piece, the revealed truth of *The Book* holds absolute sway. And it may be argued that institutional Christianity made a radical mistake in its failure to interpret revelation with a more mature understanding that would have prevented the Great Split.

> He therefore who wishes to rejoice without doubt in regard to the truths underlying phenomena must know how to devote himself to experiment. For authors write many statements, and people believe them through reasoning which they formulate without experience. Their reasoning is wholly false.
>
> Roger Bacon, *Opus majus*

The way of thinking that characterises science in its modern form had its origins in the 16th century. It was something that developed slowly and gradually, involving countless people, each adding an increment, each building on what had been discovered before. One of the most significant early figures was the Franciscan Roger Bacon (1214-1294).[6] Roger Bacon's most lasting contribution was his insistence that creation operated through natural causes that could be elucidated from careful

Roger Bacon

scrutiny of the evidence before us – experiment in other words. But in spite of his emphasis on the central importance of experiment to prove if an idea were true, if it corresponded to what happened in reality, Bacon did little experimenting himself. His mind was endlessly at work coming up with ingenious ideas about how things worked, especially to do with light (most of them false it has to be said). This is partly because it was difficult technically at this time to set up experiments: and it shows how painfully cumulative and stepwise was the accumulation of truth about reality.

Galileo Galilei (1564-1642)

The two great names associated with the development of scientific thinking as we recognise it today are Galileo Galilei and

Isaac Newton. Galileo's great contribution was his emphasis on experimental proof. Hearsay or instinct were insufficient, they can mislead. It never occurred to people to seek experimental proof – you could reason everything out, as if it were a theorem in mathematics. His most famous experiments concerned gravity. He demonstrated that – contrary to instinct and common sense – heavy and light objects fall at the same rate. We have all

Galileo Galilei

read about the famous experiment at the Leaning Tower of Pisa which demonstrates another very important aspect of the experimental method: repeatability (actually it wasn't Galileo who conducted it but one of his opponents, in order to prove him wrong). The most striking repetition of the Pisa experiment was carried out by astronauts on the moon when they dropped a hammer and a feather, and before our still astonished eyes they fell to the ground at the same time. Dropping weights from leaning towers was one thing. In a rather different league as far as the church authorities of the day were concerned was Galileo's enthusiastic embrace and further elaboration of Copernicus' new model of a heliocentric universe – with the sun rather than the earth at the centre – which led to one of the first great clashes between science and religion. Such a notion seemed to threaten God's role in the scheme of things and led to Galileo's arrest and confinement.[7]

> Philosophy is written in this grand book, the universe, which stands continually open to our gaze. But the book cannot be understood unless one first learns to comprehend the language and read the letters in which it is composed. It is written in the language of mathematics, and its characters are triangles, circles, and geometrical figures without which it is humanly impossible to understand a word of it.
>
> *Galileo Galilei*

Isaac Newton

Copernicus

Isaac Newton (1642-1727)

Newton too was a great experimenter, but his greater contribution was to demonstrate that the behaviour of things is governed by laws that are literally universal: they apply everywhere, not just on earth, but out there in the universe, governing the stars as well as our cars – and at all times, not just today. Most famously he realised that the pull of gravity which makes an apple fall is the same force that keeps the moon in orbit, or the earth in orbit around the sun. And it applies to the stars themselves. The universe is governed not by capricious gods; it runs in accordance with predetermined, inviolable laws – laws that can be discovered if we are smart and skilful enough to design and carry out the right experiments to find out what they are. And that is the science of physics in a nutshell: the search for universal laws that can be discovered by carrying out a succession of ever more subtle and ingenious experiments.

One of Newton's most important contributions was his discovery of inertia: 'Any object will keep moving in a straight line at constant speed (or will stay still) unless it is pushed or pulled by a force.' This is Newton's first law of motion. It isn't obvious. Galileo thought circular motion was the natural way for objects to behave – look at the moon, the planets. Reality is not always what it appears to be. An impressive demonstration of inertia took place in 1640 when Pierre Gassendi took a slave galley out into the Mediterranean, rowed flat out, then climbed to the top of the mast and dropped a series of balls that fell straight down relative to the ship because they were moving at the same speed as the ship.

A thought experiment

Imagine you are watching a train hurtling along at 100 mph. Somebody jumps out the window as you are watching. Now imagine that at this very second the train – just the train – becomes invisible to you (although it is still there). What will you see? This gives us a further glimpse of the importance of *frames of reference* – and if you can imagine the jumper confined within four windowless walls *he won't notice his forward motion.*

The image of the universe that emerged from Newtonian mechanics was that of a gigantic and endlessly intricate piece of clockwork, with God as the omnipotent clockmaker.

From this Newton moved on to investigate orbital theory. Why the earth revolves, or the moon, is that its tendency to move in a straight line is deflected by gravity. And you can measure the amount and then predict on the basis of that accurate

---

Newton's first law of motion

Any object will keep moving in a straight line at constant speed (or will stay still) unless it is pushed or pulled by a force.

Newton's second law of motion

When a force is applied to an object moving in a straight line at constant speed, its velocity changes at a rate proportional to the force that is applied, and in the direction that the force is applied (i.e. it accelerates): $f \div m = a$.

Newton's third law of motion

Whenever a force is applied to an object, it pushes back with an equal and opposite force (the reaction).

---

measurement. For example, Newton worked out by experiment that when an apple falls, it falls 16 feet in the first second. He was able to measure the amount by which the moon is pulled or deflected by the earth: it's 1/20 of an inch in a second. That's 1/3800 of the pull on the apple. But the moon is 60 times further from the centre of the earth than the apple is, so the pull is 60 times weaker (3800 is 60 x 60). So gravity obeys an inverse square law. It is weakened by the square of its distance. This same law explains the orbit of the planets.

> I do not know what I may appear to the world, but to myself I seem to have been only like a boy playing on the sea-shore, and diverting myself in now and then finding a smoother pebble or a prettier shell than ordinary, whilst the great ocean of truth lay all undiscovered before me.
>
> *Isaac Newton*

The nature of light

Newton then set out to explain light in the same mechanical way. He thought of light as a stream of tiny invisible particles moving in straight lines. In fact he was only partly right, but so great was his reputation that it was the accepted explanation through the 18th century and beyond. It wasn't easy to prove him wrong at the time. In fact, a contemporary, Christiaan Huygens (1629-1695) had the correct idea but Newton's reputation eclipsed him. He thought light consisted of vibrations in some all-pervading medium that filled the universe. Both ideas could explain the classic behaviour of light: the way it was reflected by shiny surfaces and refracted when it entered a different medium. But according to Newton's calculations, it would travel faster if it entered a denser medium, whereas according to Huygens, it would travel more slowly – when it entered water from air, for instance. In the 18th century it wasn't possible to test this accurately by experiment. But when it did become possible Huygens was proved to be right. Light does travel in waves (although it is particulate).

The wave nature of light was demonstrated by Thomas Young with surprisingly simple equipment: three cards – two side by side with parallel slits and the third, with a pinhole, in front of these two. The pinhole allowed light from a single source to reach the two slits. When they emerge from the slits the beams diverge, and where they meet they produce patterns exactly like in water, or like sound waves travelling in the air. But what is vibrating? The man who elucidated that was Michael Faraday who introduced the notion of a field of force, which he famously demonstrated with the familiar magnet and iron filings experiment.[8]

> The idea that [the sciences], or any narrow group of them, could furnish the whole purpose of human life, will probably strike us as extremely strange. Since its effect is to tear the human faculties apart, divorcing intellect from feeling, spirit, action and bodily perception, it denies even to intellect itself most of the scope which it should naturally have.
>
> Mary Midgley, *Evolution as a Religion* (2002)

Newton and Goethe

There is another interesting aspect to the quest to understand light. Newton was the first to describe in detail the way a glass prism will split light into its component colours, but he was not the only one. Johann Wolfgang von Goethe (1749-1832) is better remembered today as one of the greatest figures in the history of European literature, but he was also a scientist who made significant discoveries in anatomy and botany. He too carried out intensive studies on the nature of light, in order to refute Newton's explanation of the prism experiment, which Goethe considered to be a simplification of what really happens. He went to painstaking lengths to demonstrate this, and a long and bitter dispute ensued. Goethe's own theory is very complicated and hard to follow, but at the heart of it is his sense that there is more to light than this. This debate is central to an adequate understanding of the nature of science and of the way our senses apprehend the evidence. There is more to say about light, about the experience of light, than the fact that it is refracted by a prism into its component colours, each with a different wavelength. It is as though the immeasurable experience has nothing to do with the measurable 'explanation'. The prism demonstrates one aspect of the behaviour of light; this behaviour is part of the nature of light, but it is *not* light. Is everything about the rainbow explained by knowing its colours are produced when light is refracted through raindrops? Is the experience of colour, the beauty of it, an irrelevant aspect of reality? Is my response to it to be explained away in some similarly measurable fashion? Or to take a chemical example: what is water? Water is H_2O, a fascinating molecule whose chemical properties are well understood. But the physics and chemistry of water don't describe the full reality of water, the existential dimension to its being. What about the being of waterfalls and waves and snow? Are the music, art and poetry, through which we attempt to articulate our human response, no more than meaningless froth?

> All theory, dear friend, is gray, but the golden tree of life springs ever green.
>
> Goethe, *Faust*, Part 1

Whatever about the being of physical and chemical entities, it is when we apply our reductionist philosophy to living things that it becomes especially insidious. When we dissect a bird or a plant, the mechanism whereby its heart beats or its flowers communicate with pollinators can be discovered: and while my

> I caught this morning morning's minion, king-
>   dom of daylight's dauphin, dapple-dawn-drawn Falcon, in
>   his riding
>   Of the rolling level underneath him steady air, and striding
> High there, how he rung upon the rein of a wimpling wing
> In his ecstasy! then off, off forth on swing,
>   As a skate's heel sweeps smooth on a bow-bend: the hurl
>   and gliding
>   Rebuffed the big wind. My heart in hiding
> Stirred for a bird, – the achieve of, the mastery of the thing!
>
> Brute beauty and valour and act, oh, air, pride, plume, here
>   Buckle! AND the fire that breaks from thee then, a billion
> Times told lovelier, more dangerous, O my chevalier!
>
>   No wonder of it: shéer plód makes plough down sillion
> Shine, and blue-bleak embers, ah my dear,
>   Fall, gall themselves, and gash gold-vermilion.
>   Gerard Manley Hopkins, *The Windhover* (1918)

understanding of its physiology and biochemistry can greatly enhance my appreciation of the bird, it misses altogether the thrill of the mind and spirit embodied in that muscle, bone and nerve. The beauty of the robin's song can never be adequately expressed in decibel equations.

However, taking their lead from René Descartes (1596-1650)[9] many scientists came to believe that animals are mere machines, incapable of feeling pain, pleasure or other emotions in any way that can be compared to ours. The mind of animals is something about which we will have much more to say later, but for the moment we will be content to slot this attitude to life into its historical context.

The progress of science has accelerated enormously in recent decades, both in terms of the number of people engaged in it and the sophistication of the resources available to them. The progress of our understanding of the creation in the last 50 years has been spectacular, and in many areas way beyond anything that could have been predicted 50 years ago. By the same token, it is likely that progress in the next 50 years will be even more spectacular.

Measurement and number
The scientific method requires us to confine our evidence to what (in the broad sense) we can see, and to formulate our hypotheses on that basis. We then translate our observation into careful description; accurate measurement using rods and clocks of all sorts is central to this, and these measurements are recorded numerically and their relationships expressed through mathematics, the science of number, which is a world that few readers will be familiar with. This is more difficult than you might think, because it took a long time to invent accurate measuring devices. Accurate measurement of *volume*, for example, had to await the invention of suitable glassware, of *time* the development of accurate timepieces; indeed, the story of the evolution of each of these instruments is a fascinating tale of human ingenuity and endeavour.[10] (A familiar example – because it was the subject of a best-selling popular book – is the accurate measurement of longitude.)[11]

However, the scientific method as generally understood re-

THE SINGING HEART OF THE WORLD

stricts itself to what it can measure and reduce to number. This is to abstract from the ontological reality before us, other dimensions of which cannot be reduced to number. If we believe we can access and describe everything that is important by confining our attention to those aspects of creation that can be measured with rulers and clocks, we are guilty of reductionism, the belief that everything can be explained in terms of its component parts, like a machine. We are making a fundamental mistake at the outset of our enquiry into the nature of reality, and one that will distort everything we later build on our discoveries. In the prologue to his work *On Being and Essence,* Thomas Aquinas quotes Aristotle to the effect that a small error in the beginning grows enormous at the end, being magnified at every subsequent turning so that it distorts all that is built upon it subsequently, even if no further mistake is made.[12] And it is progressively more difficult to undo that error the further you progress on your misdirected journey.

Attitudes to science

In our everyday lives we constantly acknowledge the way of knowing that the scientific approach follows. We have no hesitation in flying round the world, or communicating by phone. We do not doubt the science, the understanding of how creation works, that makes these miracles possible: we just hope they have the science right! We express our faith in science every time we visit the doctor, every time we strike a match. But when the same set of intellectual procedures confronts us with something that seems to contradict our comfortably and deeply-held beliefs we may see it as a threat and want to reject it. This attitude is predominant in Islam today – as it was in Christianity until recently, and still is in certain 'fundamentalist' denominations. But we cannot pick and choose like this. The mode of enquiry that has established such concepts as the evolution of life on earth is exactly the same as that which gives us mobile phones. Evolution is as certain as the fact that the phone will work when you switch it on. In such instances, either the science is wrong, or our belief is too confined, too narrow. The former may well be true, but it is part of the methodology of science to approach ever-greater accuracy and certainty in its conclusions.

But the alternative to selective rejection does not oblige us to be unquestioningly credulous, accepting not only the discoveries of science *sensu stricto* with uncritical acceptance, but also holistic extrapolations or worldviews built on aspects of the vast multitude of partial findings which individual scientists or others may make about the broader meaning of these discoveries.

Three responses are possible to us then. We can simply refuse to accept the picture of the world that science uncovers and continue to pick and choose without facing the truth, because we place greater trust in 'revelation'. Or secondly we can have unquestioning credulity in everything that 'science' (or scientists) appears to say. Or we can embrace the discoveries of science, and undertake the journey in wisdom to integrate these into our growing understanding, our overview, of what it is all about. The scientific method is a way of knowing, grounded in human understanding of (direct) experience. It eschews hearsay, even the special form of hearsay we call revelation, because after all hearsay may or may not be true, and different modes of revelation contradict each other – or at least particular interpretations of them do. It is the exercise of our body, mind, and spirit in pursuit of a fuller understanding of creation. As such, it has added enormously to the depth and richness of our appreciation and understanding of the word of God: for it is the faith of those who believe in God that he speaks to us through creation, which we apprehend through our senses (See chapters 5 and 6).

And although it is deeply rooted in the western tradition, at its most fundamental scientific enquiry is part of the essence of being human: not something we don as a mantle (or a white coat) and take off when we leave the laboratory: it is the use of unfettered understanding and intelligence, a desire to understand God's world more fully. It is the most distinctively human thing there is about us. Science is also a communal human achievement. It belongs to all of us: not merely in the sense of standing on the shoulders of those who came before (as Newton put it),[13] but in the sense that we all share that way of being made, genetically, by virtue of our common evolutionary history. 'We [mankind],' wrote Martin Heidegger, 'are a conversation.'[14] 'The whole of science,' Albert Einstein wrote, 'is nothing more than a refinement of everyday thinking.'[15] And that is the most important thing I would like you to remember as you read through this book: that science is your way of thinking, and its disinterested pursuit leads in one direction only.

The method of science in its early stages is open to all, and is the foundation of craft. But as science goes ever deeper it takes the human mind along paths increasingly deep below the surface and ever narrower, which only few can follow. Hence the increasing specialisation and abstractness of science – but it must always retain its lifeline, the arteries that connect it to the touch of the surface, which always grounds our experience.

There is therefore a great difference between science as our quest for understanding and its use for commercial gain. Such 'scientifically proven' claims as (for example) that athletes will run faster on SpeediSquash, or this skin product will get rid of wrinkles and make you look young again etc, are not couched in the careful language of science. Our suspicion of science is justified when it is hijacked for commercial gain or in support of a perspective that eschews religion, or when the ever-more precise insights it provides into the working of creation are used for wrong ends. But sometimes our suspicion or fear of science are due rather to our reluctance to work with the deeper perspectives on divinity it challenges us with.

Science and morality

Science is as successful as it is because it works, because it makes life better or more comfortable for us. And it has transformed the human condition. One of the many difficulties is that it is blind and it is amoral. It is enormously beneficial when it enables us to pull ourselves or others up from abject poverty or starvation to the golden mean of well-being, to modest comfort. But it does not provide us with the wisdom to stop as the good life which science and technology provide us with drifts into abject, materialistic affluence.

That is one major problem. Another is the power that it puts at our fingertips. The hand in question here is not that of a human race imbued with wisdom and compassion and a sense of balance, but a human race in whose ears the recently-slammed gates of paradise are still ringing while God fumes with frustration among his apple trees. The scientist can be a saint or a sinner. Most are a mixture, haloes and horns like the rest of us. Bernard Shaw said of the great Russian physiologist Ivan Petrovich Pavlov (Nobel Prize 1904) that he would 'boil babies alive just to see what happens' – a true disciple of Descartes, who believed animals were simply elaborate machines, bundles of stimuli and responses, incapable of feeling pain. Or take Fritz Haber (Nobel Prize 1918), who in the first decade of the last century discovered how to make ammonia from nitrogen in the atmosphere and laid the foundation of the modern fertiliser industry. One result was that Germany never ran out of nitrates for ammunition production during World War I. Haber, who was an extremely patriotic German and a great scientist, then threw all his energies into developing the use of gas as a weapon during the war, directing the first use of chlorine and mustard gas.[16] At the other end of the scale are scientists of the calibre of Albert Einstein, a wonderful human being, one of the greatest scientists of all time. When the first atomic bombs were dropped on Japan and he saw the power he had unleashed and how it could be used to destroy, Einstein wrote 'If I had known [what would be done with my work] I would have been a locksmith.'

The failure of the scientific enterprise
For all its thrilling success and the way it has transformed our lives, the scientific enterprise has failed in three fundamental ways. First of all, in the limited way in which rationality is applied: to isolated facets of reality, applying the knowledge gained in techniques that threaten disaster because they are not applied holistically, with an eye to their impact on the earth as a whole. Solutions that are purely technological, in the words of Wendell Berry, cause 'a ramifying series of new problems, the only limiting criterion being, apparently, that the new solutions should arise beyond the purview of the expertise that produced the solution – as, in agriculture, industrial solutions to the problem of production have invariably caused problems of maintenance, conservation, economics, community health, etc, etc.'[17] Take, for example, the effect of industrial activity that is driven by the energy from fossil fuel. A holistic approach would take all the effects of burning coal or oil into account from the start: i.e.

into the account book that reckons up the true cost in terms of its impact upon all the functions and values of nature it affects. Or take the way advances in medicine prolong life and permit the human population to explode at the rate it has been growing in recent decades without at the same time taking account of the environmental impact and without making provision in advance so that it is possible for each to live a dignified, fulfilled life that does not compromise the fulfillment of other lives.

Secondly, because of the degree to which we ignore the most fundamental function of scientific reasoning – at least viewed from the perspective of these pages – which is to broaden and deepen human understanding and appreciation of creation: which is most immediately a failure of education, but ultimately, of course, a loss of the belief that this is its prime reason in the first place. 'Science is about cultivating a perpetual condition of wonder in the face of something that forever grows one step richer and subtler than our latest theory about it. It is about reverence, not mastery.'[18]

And thirdly – but not unrelated to the first two – the almost total concentration on developing and applying science for economic ends primarily: providing people with goods they don't need, certainly cannot understand the working of, but, the important thing, they must pay for. This is the substitution of a new, highly reliable form of magic for older, less lucrative ones. And at the same time our failure to devote our minds and resources to areas of research that do not bring in money: so that little research is likely to be done on the diseases of people who cannot pay if these diseases do not plague the rich also; or the improvement of food crops that would lift the lives of the poor if they do not also appear on our supermarket shelves; or sustainable energy techniques if they threaten the profitability of existing technologies, however polluting they be. On the other hand, science has greatly magnified the problems of humanity through the development of ever-increasingly sophisticated technology for weaponry, and for the support of affluence: 'That even in the third millennium billions are invested in the all-embracing armaments industry instead of in the fight against poverty, hunger, disease, and illiteracy, goes against all reason.'[19] Our overweening application of science to the wrong ends teeters so close to the brink of sustainability that it is in doubt whether the civilisation we so take for granted can survive this 21st century.[20]

How dulled our sense of appreciation is in danger of becoming! Not only confronted with the wonder and majesty of all that the unfolding of the cosmos has made part of our experience – the wonders of the natural world in all its manifestations – but in the face of the achievements of cultural ingenuity that enfold our lives at every moment of every day: paper and woven things, metal and plastic, electronics – of which we understand nothing more than our ancestors understood the happenings they attributed to magic and the gods – except that we should understand them if science were doing its job, or rather if we were making the use we are meant to make of these discoveries.

CHAPTER 2

The Architecture of Creation: Cosmos

> The universe, the solar system, and planet earth in themselves
> and in their evolutionary emergence constitute for the human
> community the primary revelation of that ultimate mystery
> whence all things emerge into being.
> Thomas Berry: *Twelve Principles for Understanding the Universe*
> *and the Role of the Human in the Universe Process*

The material of creation

Science is evidence-based, so it remains anchored to the real. It
has splintered into various disciplines because the growth of
knowledge has made specialisation necessary, but what they all
have in common is that they are based on what reason can
extract from the world of experience. So chemistry and geology
study the material of which the world is made, and astronomy
studies the same material a very long way off. Physics and
mathematics study the laws that govern this material. Biology
studies life, but life is made of the same material. If you like,
physics, chemistry, biology, psychology study matter at progressively higher levels of integration or organisation. New
properties emerge at each higher level, but each level still obeys
the laws of the level below.

In this chapter we will look at how science, and in particular
the discoveries of the last hundred years, have contributed to
our understanding of the nature of the universe itself: its origins,
its make-up, the processes at work in it. Indeed, it is more than a
mere 'contribution', because we owe our understanding of the
unfolding of the cosmos entirely to what science has revealed.
The new picture of the formation and ongoing evolution of the
universe is awe-inspiring beyond words. A brief account is
given below, but to begin to grasp what is going on in a way that
is emotionally, psychologically and spiritually – as well as intellectually – satisfying, you need to see the stunning imagery of
the ballet of cosmic evolution generated from the data gathered
by the Hubble telescope since its launch in 1990.[1]

This is the ultimate creation story. It differs from all other creation tales in that it is not a myth. It is suffused with mystery, but it's not myth. It is grounded in the reality of what actually happened, still happens. Myths are created from intuition and imagination, and they differ from culture to culture, but they are not grounded in the truth of material reality. This New Creation Story is created not through imagination and intuition, but by using the most distinctively human part of what we are, our intellect. When we hear the story, it is important to remember this – even though it is told to us with imagination and intuition – as it is by Brian Swimme and Tom Berry, or by Nellie McLoughlin.[2] This creation story is true on an altogether different level, a level that brings together all creation stories and rises above them. But it is science, spun with the method of science, anchored to reality and forged through experiment and proof: and always being refined and expanded.

The nature and scale of the universe

By the time of Christ it had been established scientifically that the earth is a sphere and its diameter had been determined mathematically. But the evidence for how it fitted together with everything else in the universe – stars, planets, the space in which they moved – was very limited: there were no telescopes remember. What limited evidence there was, coupled with philosophical and theological presumption, seemed to place the earth at the centre of the universe, with the various heavenly bodies arranged in a series of concentric spheres.

In the western tradition this geocentric view was elaborated in the second century AD from centuries of earlier work by Greek astronomers into what came to be known as the Ptolemaic model, after the Alexandrian astronomer Claudius Ptolemaeus. It survived for a thousand years, but the geocentric model was the first great cornerstone of the old 'accepted wisdom' to be shattered by the scientific approach, through the careful calculation and observation of Tycho Brahe, Copernicus and Galileo (among others).[3] Their work led to the development of a hypothesis that more adequately explained the new data: and so the concept of the heliocentric universe was born and elaborated over the centuries that followed. This was concerned with the work-

The Geocentric Cosmos: Schematic representation of the view of the universe that prevailed from its formulation by Ptolemy in the first century AD until its overthrow by Copernicus in the 16th century. The spherical earth is at the centre, surrounded by a series of ten concentric spheres where the moon, sun and planets reside at varying distances. The outer spheres beyond are inhabited by the stars, including the special groups that constitute the Zodiac. Outside this concentric series of spheres is *coelum empireum habitaculum dei et omnium electorum*: the great empyrean where God and all those who have been chosen reside. This version is from Andreas Cellarius' *Harmonia Macrocosmica* (1660/61).

ings of our solar system more or less exclusively: but indeed, earth is the merest speck even within the solar system itself.

For a long, long time the universe beyond the solar system was imagined to be little more than the starry background to our corner of creation, where most of the exciting things happened. It is only over the last hundred years or so that we have come to see how infinitesimally small our solar system is. The diameter of the sun is 109 times that of the earth (which is 12,756km): if we reduce its size to that of a basketball then the earth is a marble 27.5m away. On this scale the nearest star to us (Alpha Centauri) is something like 3,400km or so away. There are something like 100 billion stars in our small island galaxy, the Milky Way: which (to use Bill Bryson's unforgettable comparison) is about the number of grains of rice that could be squeezed into a warehouse the size of a cathedral. Each of these stars burns at 10 million degrees, releasing the energy equivalent to a thousand billion hydrogen bombs going off every second. And in the observable universe there are maybe 400 billion galaxies. Each speck seen through Hubble represents not a star, but a galaxy. The size of a 10 cent piece held at arm's length covers more than 100,000 galaxies.

The lives of stars

As scientists we don't know anything about what was there before the beginning, because there is no evidence. The evidence we do have takes us back in time to a moment when everything exploded into existence, came into being, out of what is helplessly called a 'singularity' at the beginning of time.

15 billion years ago our universe did not exist. Then, some 14.7 billion years ago, a process astrophysicists call 'vacuum fluctuation' caused a singularity. Our universe grew from a tiny volume whose density approached what is considered to be the theoretical maximum (known as the Planck density: 5.1 x 1096 kilograms per cubic metre – a trillion solar masses compressed to the size of a proton): itself it may be the result of the gravitational collapse of a pre-existing universe: in effect a rebound rather than a 'bang.' The human mind just cannot get itself around the reality of what happened at the very beginning: that the entire universe came into being out of a speck equal to 10-20 times the size of a proton. William Blake could never have realised how impossibly truly 'a world' might exist 'in a grain of sand' – that in fact, the entire universe could unfold from a mass little bigger than that. From the 'explosion' of that infinitely dense, marble-sized singularity, matter and light, space and time unfolded. If space had unfurled even a trillionth of one percent more slowly, it would have collapsed. If it had emerged more rapidly, then the constituents would have been too separated for anything interesting to happen. The four basic forces were established within seconds: the gravitational force, electromagnetism and the two nuclear forces. Everything that happens afterwards depends absolutely on the precise strength of these forces. If the gravitational force had been even slightly different, no galaxies could have formed. With even a slightly different strong interaction, all the stars that subsequently formed would quickly have exploded.[4]

The universe thrives on the edge of a knife. If it increased its strength of expansion it would blow up; if it decreased its strength of expansion it would collapse. The Milky Way also thrives at the edge of a knife. Decrease its gravitational bonding and all the stars scatter; increase it and the galaxy collapses upon itself.[5]

Nothing was permanent in the beginning. All particles – quarks, electrons, muons, photons, neutrons and their antiparticles – cascaded into existence, interacted with other particles, and then disappeared back into non-existence (we can – albeit very loosely indeed – think of matter as 'energy at rest'). At first, there could be no *interaction* between particles. But if the process of unfurling had been slower, the particles would have interacted with each other until all that remained was a ball of iron.

Within its first second, the universe had expanded to the point where particles could continue to exist. The initial fireball now settled down as baryons and simple nuclei. For the first 380,000 years the expanding universe was too hot for nuclei and free electrons to combine to form neutral atoms of hydrogen, and the continuous and all-pervasive scattering by the free electrons prevented the escape of photons. But once hydrogen formed the photons were able to escape, and the universe exploded with light. This formation of atoms could not have happened earlier. *Nor could it have been predicted from the properties of what was there before*. By a process we will see over and over as matter evolves to ever greater levels of complexity, organisation and interaction, there is a new 'flowering' of the basic laws.

Fluctuations in the distribution of matter and energy caused matter and energy to gather as the universe expanded: i.e. expansion was not even, giving uniform matter and energy spread evenly throughout space-time. This fluctuation caused matter to constellate into a trillion separate clouds of hydrogen and helium. Density waves within these 'lacy veils' of galaxies shocked clouds of hydrogen and helium into condensing rapidly to form *stars*, and the universe once more burst into radiance.[6] Each cloud held together as the universe continued its expansion.

On one of these gossamer filaments hung the Virgo cluster, a self-containing gathering of a thousand separate galaxies. Bonded to this cluster were a great many clusters, including one pinwheel formation of two dozen galaxies having two poles: the Andromeda galaxy on one side and our own home, the Milky Way galaxy on the other. Within the Milky Way, we live in a stellar system twenty-eight light years from the galactic centre, two-thirds of the distance to the edge. Our sun is one of the hundred billion stars that the Milky Way swirls around itself, each of them spinning about in a bonded relationship with every other one. And the Milky Way remains bonded to all one hundred billion galaxies of the cosmos ...[7]

As each newborn star condenses it begins to 'collapse' under gravitation. Hydrogen collapses into protons and then these combine to helium nuclei to stave off the pressure. As this fuel is used up the helium can transform or condense to carbon and other higher order nuclei to sustain the star against the crushing pressure of gravity. After a million or several billion years the star runs out of the resources it needs to stave off gravitational collapse. It then explodes as a *supernova*. How this happens depends on the mass of the star. If it is big enough there is a massive collapse to form a *pulsar* (a super dense mass of neutrinos), or goes all the way down to a *black hole*, a 'naught entity'. Nothing but a black cinder remains. The nearest black hole to ourselves is at the centre of the Milky Way.

As the star collapses, its wispy neutrinos rush out in all directions, blowing away the outer layers of the star, where the carbon, oxygen, nitrogen and other elements are concentrated. The stellar dust, rich in these new elements, journeys through space to be caught up in the next chapter of the universe story. A supernova is briefly as bright as many tens or even hundreds of billions of suns. In our galaxy a star explodes in a brilliant supernova once every hundred years or so (the last one was seen by Kepler in 1604). But over time 200 million stars have exploded in our galaxy, scattering all the heavier elements into space. Had the balance of primary forces at the beginning been differently established, supernovas would not occur, and larger atoms would not be scattered across the universe.

The process can be repeated, maybe several times, so that

stars of second, third and higher generations are made of fundamentally different galactic matter than the early stars.

> In the Milky Way galaxy 4.5 billion years ago, the disc of stars was relatively rich in all the elements. Rushing through this sea were the two great spokes of the density arms whose velocity at the edge of the Milky Way was 20 miles per second. As these invisible waves spun, they drew forth millions of star bursts, each new star with its own particular destiny.[8]

In our area of space-time the density wave passed through every 100 million years. The most massive stars exploded as supernovas, enriching interstellar matter. By the time of our sun's birth, perhaps 200 passes of this star-making wave had occurred.

> Eventually a wave swept through that triggered the burst of some ten thousand stars all at once. This cluster ranged from blue giants with surface temperatures in the range of fifty thousand degrees, able to burn so brightly but exploding after only a million years, all the way down to small cool stars with surface temperatures of only a couple of thousand degrees, but capable of burning for hundreds of billions of years. Ten thousand stars, and each had a different fate determined by the waves fracturing the initial cloud. One of these subclouds was destined to become the sun of our solar system. This subcloud to begin with was 5 million times the size of the sun it would eventually become.[9]

It took hundreds of thousands of years for the sun to condense to its present size, going through a sequence of chemical changes as pressure and temperature rose. At ten million degrees, hydrogen began to burn to helium. The sun was born. Not all the gas went to the core of the new star. Around the sun, a disc of the original subcloud spun, a whirling disc of elements, a leftover cool remnant, one-hundredth the size of the sun itself. From this the planets condensed.

Supernova activity and the creation of new stars are only possible in spiral galaxies. It cannot take place in elliptical or irregular galaxies, or in globular clusters. And there were billions of spiral galaxies scattered throughout the universe. It was in one such spiral – the Milky Way – 4.5 billion years ago, near a star coming out of a recent supernova explosion, that our solar system was formed.

The Sun

Our sun is a medium-sized star, powered by the fusion of helium. Other thermonuclear reactions occur within the dense, high temperatures in the depths of stars, producing heavier elements such as carbon, oxygen and still heavier elements. The sun is in a plasma state, where electrons and nuclei are separated into a conducting fluid of elementary particles. Tremendous gravitational forces result that should collapse the plasma, but this is balanced by the gas pressure of the plasma below, generating a hydrostatic balance which maintains it the way it is. At the heart of the sun – or any comparable star – the pressure is a billion atmospheres and the temperature over 10 million degrees C. The sun has been pouring out its energy for over 5 billion years, and will probably do so for as long again.

Eventually the core of a star begins to run out of fuel and it starts to shrink. This releases gravitational potential energy that is absorbed by the outer layers, causing them to heat up and to expand to huge proportions (in fact, the outer layers are relatively cool – and therefore redder – because of the now much larger surface area). It has become a red giant.

At some point a chemical process known as the 'triple-alpha process' abruptly sets in throughout the core, involving three colliding helium nuclei. This results in the creation of progressively heavier elements and reverses the shrinkage of the stellar core, so that the outer layers of the star collapse inwards, heating up as they go and ending the first red giant phase after about a billion years. Over a few hundred million years thereafter it expands to red giant status again and again as new nuclear processes fuse higher elements, gradually exhausting its fuel. Eventually a stage comes (usually) where (the core being now almost totally converted to iron) the core collapses, releasing such huge amounts of gravitational energy that the star explodes, sending its outer layers hurtling into space, enriching the interstellar medium with heavier elements that will con-

41

tribute to the formation of the next generation of stars with the elements that form rocky worlds. Every atom in our body with the exception of hydrogen, was manufactured countless eons ago by nuclear reactions inside a star and spread across space in a supernova explosion. We, and everything else that lives and breathes, are literally made of stardust.

The dying star then collapses, and what happens next depends on its mass. The internal pressure supports the outer layers, and the bigger the original star the smaller its radius now is. These stars are incredibly dense (in the densest stars known each cubic centimetre of material would weigh a hundred million tonnes). Where the parent star exceeds a minimum of three times the mass of our sun, the interior cannot support the mass of the outer layers and so it collapses to almost nothing, and is so dense that its escape velocity (which depends on the gravity) is so high that even light cannot escape and is permanently trapped: it has become a black hole. This will not happen below the three solar masses limit. Our sun will in 5 billion years evolve to a red giant engulfing everything as far as the orbit of Venus, incinerating earth in a red inferno.

The formation of our solar system

Our solar system probably formed when a nebula of interstellar gas and dust began to condense about 4.5-5 billion years ago. This swirling nebula was disturbed some 4.6 billion years ago by the explosion of a nearby star, and the shock waves sent it spinning slightly, initiating collapse by the nebula under its own gravity – the end of one star triggering the formation of another. As it collapsed, its initially slight rotational speed increased (like a pirouetting ice skater bringing in her arms). The process converted the nebula into a rapidly spinning disc (all the planets lie in the same plane for this reason). This continued for 100 million years or so, and gradually the gravitational potential energy of the nebula was converted to thermal energy and our spinning protosun formed, quickly reaching 2000°K at the centre, and as low as 50°K (=-223°C) at the edges. Accretion of material formed the terrestrial planets and their moons (by gravitational and electrical forces). Planets vary in chemical composition in accordance with size and distance from the sun.

On Mercury, Venus, Mars and Pluto all geological activity soon came to a halt. They froze. Because of their small size they are not big enough for gravitation to give rise to processes able to break down rocks once they had formed. On Jupiter, Saturn, Uranus and Neptune there was – is – too much gravity for rocks to form at all. They are still balls of elemental material in gaseous form. Only earth has the right size for continued geological activity, and *only earth is at the right distance from the sun for a temperature at which complex molecules can form.*

The stately motions of today's earth are the legacy of that swirling birth. Our planet turns on its axis each day at an average of about 1000 kilometres an hour and circles the sun once a year at a hundred times this speed. And at the same time our entire solar system circles the centre of the Milky Way at 800,000 kilometres an hour.

CHAPTER THREE

The Architecture of Creation: Chemistry

There are 92 different naturally-occurring *elements* in the universe, all with different weights and properties. The smallest particle of an element is an *atom*. Atomic theory in its present-day form traces its beginnings to the work of John Dalton around 1800 (although in fact the Jesuit mathematician and astronomer R. G. Boscovich (1711-1787) put forward an essentially similar idea before this). Because they are too small to weigh as we would weigh larger things, the weight of the smallest atom (which is hydrogen) is used as the unit, and others are multiples of that. The atomic weight of nitrogen, for instance, is 14, which means its atom is 14 times as heavy as that of hydrogen.[1] Caesium, with an atomic weight of 132.9, has the largest atom – all of .0000005mm ($5x10^7$mm) across. It would take ten million atoms side by side to stretch across the gap between two of the points on the serrated edge of a postage stamp.[2]

Atoms of the same or different elements combine to form *molecules*. Everything that exists (everything *that we know of* that is: see below, page 46) is made up of atoms and molecules. Living things are made of very complex molecules (these are the subject matter of organic chemistry). The sun and moon and planets are all made of the same elements, mainly the very lightest ones. The only situation where heavier elements can form is under the unimaginable conditions found in the explosive supernovae that bring the life of certain stars to an end (see page 39).

Atoms, however, are not what they were named to be: *atomos* means indivisible. At first we thought of atoms as miniature billiard balls of different sizes, and this seemed to square with the experimental evidence – until one experiment showed the inadequacy of this picture and it was back to the drawing board for atomic physics, and the discovery of a deeper, unsuspected layer.[3] We then discovered that each atom consists of a central *nucleus* around which one or more negatively-charged particles called *electrons* circle at immense speed like planets around a sun. The nucleus is made up of much more massive positively-charged particles called *protons* equal in number to the electrons, and (except for hydrogen) a more or less equal number of *neutrons* (which carry no electrical charge). But most of the atom is empty space: the proportion of the size of the nucleus to the size of the electron cloud is that of a grain of sand in the middle of the Albert Hall.[4] At the beginning of the last century Albert Einstein developed his theory of Special Relativity, the most shocking revelation of which is the enormous amount of energy it takes to hold an atom together, because it's a tightly-held cluster of screamingly antagonistic sub-atomic particles. The equation calculating this is perhaps the most famous in the whole of science: the energy equals the object's mass times the speed of light squared ($e = mc^2$). *A kilogram of anything holds enough energy to boil a hundred billion kettles – or destroy a city.*

Nor was that the end of it. We now know that the 'elementary' particles are themselves made of smaller things – but what does 'thing' mean anymore? We give these smaller things names, which supports our human tendency to think of them as 'things'. In what has come to be known as the 'standard model' in particle physics, painstakingly put together over the last century, there are 17 elementary particles. A newer theory postulates elementary particles not as points at all but as tiny 'strings' in the order of 10^{-35}m long (this is 1 preceded by 35 noughts, in front of which there is a decimal point). The different patterns of vibration of these strings are responsible for the different particles we observe. This is a very strange picture compared to the clarity of the billiard-balls. It is not really a picture at all, because it is literally unimaginable – not possible to imagine – and yet it is comprehensible to our minds, but only in the blind language of mathematics. To take all this still further beyond the realm of the imaginable, string theory requires seven dimensions in addition to the four familiar ones we have already – the three spatial dimensions and time![5]

Individual quantum particles can be in two (or three, or four) places at the one time – or maybe spread out throughout some region, perhaps wriggling about like a wave. How reliable is our imagination at trying to picture any of this when some physical theorists advise us to abandon the very notion of reality when we are considering phenomena at the scale of particles, atoms or even molecules – so far removed from what we are used to is quantum 'reality'.[6]

All of this only applies to the matter that we can, in the extended sense the reach of science allows us to, sense and measure. We now think this visible atomic matter only accounts for 4% of the universe by weight. 22% is thought to be 'dark matter' of unknown identity, and the remaining 74% is described as 'dark energy' and is thought to be responsible for the acceleration that caused the cosmos to begin to expand more rapidly than gravity can pull it together 5 billion years ago.[7]

The search for the ultimate nature of reality was all about the search, on progressively deeper levels, for the fundamental particles.[8] And so we think of the electron as a billiard ball with measurable position and velocity. But we find that the familiar concepts with which we anchor our conception and discussion of reality do not apply to the quantum world. An electron does not necessarily have a particular position or speed, nor a particular path. Yet this is the only image our language provides us with – and it necessarily contains assumptions that do not correspond with what is really going on. The notion we have in our heads about what a particle is carries assumptions that do not apply at the ultimate depth of focus, where it seems that what is going on is more adequately (but still in our limited human way) described by a fundamental symmetry and symmetry breaking. The 'particles' may be more correctly described as processes rather than objects.

If we do arrive at a Grand Unified Theory it will be a wonderful intellectual achievement. Knowing how the 'machinery' works in this more holistic manner may increase our ability to manipulate and control. But it will not answer the questions that our experience of reality at the macro level of clouds and waterfalls, leaves and beetles, joy and love and pain face us with every day.

Chemical evolution and diversity

As the earth's evolution progressed, its chemical diversity grew. The pre-solar nebula is thought to have contained only twelve different mineral compounds. When the sun began to burn, the increase in temperature led to the formation of around sixty compounds. The number increased to around 500 during the formation of the earth and the various geochemical processes that followed, doubling to around 1,000 when the mechanism of plate tectonics got going. But it was the appearance of life 4 billion or so years ago that brought about the most tremendous efflorescence in chemical diversity, eventually boosting the number of mineral species to around 5,000.

Photosynthetic life evolved some 2 billion years ago. Not only was the composition of the earth's atmosphere and oceans, and the history of life, profoundly changed by the proliferation of oxygen that resulted, but so was earth's mineral diversity. The proliferation of oxygen led to the formation of a whole new suite of minerals formed by *oxidation* – the combination of the highly reactive oxygen with pre-existing compounds to form new ones. Nearly half of all mineral species have formed through oxidation or weathering. The appearance of animals with shells and skeletons provided an abundance of new minerals such as carbonates, and a host of other organic minerals come into being where geological processes permit the formation of coal and petroleum.[9]

The individual molecules of these minerals arrange themselves into a regular framework or lattice that finds expression in the crystalline form of the visible specimen we find in the rock in which it formed, or hold in our hand: each with its unique and distinctive suites of characteristics – crystal form and cleavage, hardness, symmetry, colour and lustre, in every conceivable hue and with the most varied geometries.[10] It is an aspect of creation's diversity that has dazzled many and mesmerised not a few mineralogists who have devoted their lives to the contemplation of earth's dazzling beauty on this level, and indeed few of us are immune to the lure of precious stones. However, it is only when we visit the mineralogical section of a good museum of geology that we can appreciate the true beauty and diversity of earth's chemical structure.

CHAPTER FOUR

The Architecture of Creation: Earth

> My foothold is tenon'd and mortis'd in granite,
> I laugh at what you call dissolution,
> And I know the amplitude of time.
>
> Walt Whitman, *Song of Myself* 20

Tectonics and evolution

Understanding how the earth works is central to our understanding of evolution. The science of palaeontology, in particular, provides us with most of our direct evidence of the life forms that have lived on earth since the origin of life 4.6 or so billion years ago, and this evidence has become ever more compelling and fascinating as the earth's rocks are studied in ever greater detail and by ever more sophisticated and ingenious techniques.[1]

The only rocks we can actually see and handle are those that comprise the earth's solid crust, but geophysical measurements tell us that the earth is composed of concentric 'spheres' of material that increase in density towards the centre of the earth. Earth formed by accretion of colliding chunks of matter, and there were further collisions with other chunks of protoplanet material in the early years. Very early on in its history the impact of a giant meteorite tore away the moon, and caused much of the earth to melt. It remained molten for its first half a billion years, after which it began to form a solid crust (made of ultrabasic rock) on its surface (the oldest known rocks are some 4 billion years old). As soon as it began to stabilise, heavier elements sank towards the centre of the molten sphere – earth became a differentiated planet with chemically distinct zones.

At the centre is the core, which is mainly iron (3,470km across, about the size of Mars). This is surrounded by the dense, fluid *mantle*, which is mostly magnesium, iron, silicon and oxygen (2,900km thick). On the outside is a very thin, rocky crust, which is rich in oxygen, silicon, aluminium, calcium, potassium, sodium, and radioactive elements. The crust is 40km thick under the continents, which comprise lighter rock materials, but much thinner (about 10km) under the oceans, and made of heavier rocks such as basalt. As the earth cooled, a relatively rigid outer shell, known as the lithosphere, formed (comprising the crust and upper part of the mantle).

Dynamic processes deep in the earth, driven by heat transfer, density differences and gravity broke this outer shell into *lithospheric plates* of varying size that slowly move about at the surface at rates of centimetres per year. The energy that drives this process is the 'nuclear reactor' of the earth's core, which contains naturally-occurring radioactive elements that release enormous amounts of nuclear energy as they disintegrate. This keeps the interior very hot, and generates plumes of mantle material that rise towards the crust. Where they reach the surface the crust is pulled apart, causing a rift through which molten rock pours out onto the surface, pushing the plates to either side by a few centimetres each year. Most of these *diverging plate boundaries* are under the oceans, which is one reason it took so long to find out about them.

Now because the earth's surface is spherical, if plates are moving away from each other on some parts of its surface they must be moving towards each other elsewhere. What happens when such convergent plate boundaries meet depends on the relative density of the rocks of which they are made. There are two kinds of crust: a lighter type composed of the kind of material that makes up the continents, and the heavier kind that is generated on the ocean floor where volcanic lava flows out onto the surface and cools. Where one of the converging plates is heavier than the other it will sink beneath it, causing the lighter plate to rise as a range of mountains. The heavier plate is said to be *subducted*, and the boundary is marked by a deep trench in the ocean floor. Where the two convergent plate boundaries consist of oceanic crust, a zone of volcanic activity is generated along an *island arc* created by the tops of the submarine mountains that rise above the ocean floor. The most familiar example is the Japanese archipelago.

Where two plates of continental crust collide (though it is such a slow collision we hardly notice) neither can sink beneath the other, and so the crust buckles upwards to create a mountain range that continues to rise until the movement stops (or until it erodes at a faster rate than it rises). Where two convergent plates are moving past each other there is a deep crack in the crust called a *transform fault*, a zone of periodically very strong earthquake activity. Volcanic activity at the earth's surface is almost entirely confined to plate boundaries, as are earthquakes, caused by the slipping of one plate past the other when the strain in the crust caused by the relentless pressure of two plates grinding against each other is released, causing a sudden jerking movement.

The discovery of *plate tectonics*[2] has revolutionised the science of geology in a way comparable to the revolution in the life sciences to which the discovery and growing understanding of evolution gave rise. And it is a revolution still at its height, having only begun in the 1960s.[3] The most fundamental process that has been taking place at the surface of the earth, since it began to acquire its solid crust four billion years ago, has been the movement of plates across its surface. And although for obvious reasons the evidence becomes less clear and detailed the further back we go – because it is destroyed during subsequent re-working – we can now see that the process is cyclical – there has been a series of such movements since it all started.

Plate tectonics explains how bits of the crust that are now in one place on the earth's surface could have been somewhere different tens of millions of years ago, and somewhere else entirely hundreds of millions of years ago. For example, the crustal foundation of Ireland is made up of two units of crust, one of which was away to the north-west in early Palaeozoic time, the other to the south-east, separated by an ocean called the Iapetus Ocean which eventually closed, welding the two halves of Ireland together.[4] The breakup and convergence of continents through geological time is one of the most important influences on the evolution of life on earth.

Periodically the drift of crustal plates across earth's curved surface beings all landmasses together as a single supercontinent which eventually fragments into several separate landmasses that begin a new journey in different directions until they all coalesce once more. In other words, the earth's landmasses are locked in a stately quadrille that geologists call the Super-continent Cycle, the grandest of all the patterns in nature.[5] This has come to be called the Wilson Cycle (after the great geologist Tuzo Wilson, whose research provided some of the key insights in the development of the concept). The last supercontinent was Pangaea; the next one will take shape 250 million years from now.

CHAPTER FIVE

The Architecture of Creation: Life

> I believe a leaf of grass is no less than the journeywork of the stars,
> And the pismire is equally perfect, and a grain of sand,
>   and the egg of the wren,
> And the tree-toad is a chef-d'oeuvre for the highest,
> And the running blackberry would adorn the parlours of heaven,
> And the narrowest hinge in my hand puts to scorn all machinery,
> And the cow crunching with depress'd head surpasses any statue,
> And a mouse is miracle enough to stagger sextillions of infidels.
>   Walt Whitman, *Song of Myself* 31

In an earlier chapter we saw how, if the conditions are right, atoms will form from subatomic particles. And, again if the appropriate conditions prevail, larger atoms and eventually minerals and other compounds will form. And because the universe is so vast and long-lasting, the probability is that the conditions will be right somewhere, and perhaps in lots of places. The ways in which the atoms of different elements can combine with other atoms of the same element or of other elements are determined by the atomic structure peculiar to each – and in this regard carbon and nitrogen are particularly versatile. And it is the stupendous chemical wizardry spun around these and a handful of other elements that constitutes the physical basis of *life*.[1] The physical environment of the early earth provided conditions suitable for the formation of still more complex chemicals, including the amino acids that are the building blocks of proteins; and DNA and RNA, the amazing molecules which encode the structures and behaviour that characterise each life form and transmit these from one generation to the next, and which are common to every living thing.

But whatever about simple chemicals forming more complex ones in the way they might if the appropriate conditions of heat and pressure are provided in the laboratory, it still seems miraculous (in the true sense of the word[2]) that the many complex chemicals it requires should all come together to form the collaborative self-replicating structure that is the living cell. Surely this requires the intervention of a brilliant – perhaps omniscient? – designer from outside? This, indeed, is the traditional argument. However, it is also possible to argue that it just *happens* that way – that's the nature of things. But is it not even more 'miraculous' (at least in the derivative sense in which we commonly use the word[3]) that the potentiality to form cells is actually *built into* the different complex molecules that are required, just as the potentiality to form those complex molecules is built into the simpler atoms and molecules from which they were synthesised, and so on down to the evanescent and unimaginable quarks and leptons that are the ultimate building blocks of everything? In other words, *the potentiality for increasingly complex and information-rich entities to develop is inherent in the very structure of matter*: 'The mathematical principles of physics, in their elegant simplicity, somehow know about life and its vast complexity.'[4] Nor is that the end of the story; indeed, we are only half way. Over the last three billion years our earth has provided conditions that have permitted the progressive elaboration and diversification of the ever more complex single-celled and multicellular organisms that constitute life on earth.

The fundamental process that governs this evolution is the selection (by the conditions that prevail in its particular environment) of variations in structure or performance that increase an organisms's chances of survival, and the transmission of those favourable variations from one generation to the next. This is the basis of the principle of natural selection so brilliantly expounded by Charles Darwin in his masterly *Origin of Species* in 1859, (and independently arrived at by Alfred Russell Wallace).[5] Today we have a very good understanding of how these variations (mutations) arise and how they are transmitted from one generation to the next, as a result of advances in genetics, a science that was just about non-existent in Darwin's day, and whose origins were catalysed by the discovery of the basic laws of heredity by the Austrian Augustinian monk Gregor Mendel, and the subsequent discovery of the structures in the cell (the chromosomes) in which the hereditary material has its headquarters.[6]

The origin of life has always been one of the big questions in scientific enquiry. The fact that life will form wherever conditions permit, not just on earth but anywhere in the universe – that its possibility is inherent in matter once it reaches a particular level of chemical organisation, in other words – does not make it any less miraculous. It was such a 'great leap forward' that we must think of it as the next rung up on the ladder of increasing organisation that characterises the evolution of the material of which the universe is composed – distinguished not just by its enormously greater chemical complexity, but by its complex information processing capacity.[7]

The Great Chain

Up to modern times the living world was thought of as a great pyramid or 'Chain of Being', neatly defined in terms of increasingly valuable properties, with plants forming the base of the this-worldly part of the pyramid, the various groups of animals above this in order of closeness to ourselves, who stood above them all (in more elaborate versions of the diagram 'man' breaks down into man and woman, with the man on a higher level than the woman).[8]

At the apex was God, and between him and ourselves the various choirs of angels. This view that man is the pinnacle of earthly creation was an extension of the geocentric view that earth lay at the centre of the cosmos. Plants and animals are useful – but they are beneath us in the grand scheme of things, just as we are beneath the angels.

It was presumed that the rest of creation was placed on earth to be at the service of Man. They are the furniture on the stage on which we enact our human drama. The nature of this service was obvious with plants and animals that could be used as food, or to provide the materials for clothing and shelter. The value of creatures such as mosquitoes was less obvious but, in his *Natural Theology*, the famous nineteenth century divine William Paley suggested they might have been created in order to teach mankind the virtue of patience.[9] It was assumed, in other words, that humans were at the centre of everything in this world, and indeed in the material universe.

Evolution
> The doctrine of evolution is probably the most important revel-
> ation that has come to the world since the illuminations of
> Galileo and Copernicus.
>
> J. Howard Moore[10]

In the nineteenth century developments took place in biological
science that revolutionised our understanding of the nature of
life, in much the same way as advances in astronomy demol-
ished the simplistic geocentric view that had held sway for
millennia. By a process that echoes the way all matter in the universe evolved from that impossible-seeming kernel of material
being, that effloresced with such awesome consequences in the
Beginning of Things, we now know that all life on earth has
evolved through a common gestation within inorganic matter,
and diversified over geological time into all the creatures great
and small, plant and animal and all the myriad of smaller lives
that are neither, which people today's earth along with us. All
life on earth has a common origin. We now know, with as much
certainty as anything envisioned in human concepts and expressed in human words, that all living things have ancestors in
common, are related, in the most literal genetically-based way.
The language of Saint Francis is not a metaphor: we are all brothers and sisters. We have all evolved from a common ancestry in
ways that are increasingly well-understood. To express that in
god-language, in Teilhard de Chardin's memorable phrase, 'God
does not make things, God makes things make themselves.'[11]

This view was resisted by orthodox western religion for a
long time – of course it is still furiously resisted by many fundamentalist Christian groups, and by Islam: but it must be emphasised that there is as little doubt about the truth of organic
evolution as there is about our understanding of how electricity
and aeroplanes work (see page 29). It has been elaborated by the
same painstaking, unflinching search for the truth as revealed
by the evidence of our senses. Even reluctant Catholicism ad-
mits now that evolution is more than a hypothesis. But this does
not go nearly far enough. It needs to become central to the way
we understand creation and our place in creation and our ethical
stance towards creation.

The modern advance of astronomy has opened an awesome picture of the true scale of the universe, but of itself it allows us to continue to think of ourselves as biologically superior. Indeed, a modern William Paley could interpret it as having been created simply to demonstrate to mankind the power and grandeur of the Divinity. We could continue to see ourselves as a special creation, superior to the other creatures put here on earth to serve us, a view essentially shaped by the account of creation in the Book of Genesis, in which it took God six days to create the universe and everything in it, and which tells how God instructed us to subdue and conquer the earth, giving us 'dominion over the fish of the sea, and over the fowl of the air, and over the cattle, and over all the earth, and over every creeping thing that creepeth upon the earth.'[12] We can smile now (most of us) when we hear it put like that, but it is salutory to remember how slowly orthodox Christianity retreated from that position, and only incrementally, each increment as science inexorably undermined the prevailing notion. The organised church behaves like this all the time when confronted by a proposition that seems to threaten the tenets and values of religion.

Evolution is seen as the great arena of conflict between science and religion. 'Traditionally' we believed that the account of creation given us in Genesis (most cultures have an equally detailed mythological account) was 'true,' a true story, history. In six days, in 4004 BC, God created the universe and all that is in it. Gradually science began to see that the actual, real story was different, that all living things have developed, evolved, from a common ancestry by a concatenation of processes we call evolution, which is increasingly well understood. We can no longer think in terms of a 'Great Chain of Being' then. We must now think in terms of a Tree of Life with repeatedly dichotomous branches that has grown from one seed and developed over a time frame of several thousand million years. We humans are one small twig in a forest of related branches. On the 'twigs' nearest to us are the creatures to which we are most closely related – in our case the 'anthropoid' apes and more distantly other primates.

We are all governed by the same evolutionary processes. And we all have, fundamentally, the same make-up – in the sense that our bodies are made up of cells, and these cells have essentially the same almost unbelievably complex machinery: the biochemical pathways, the mechanism of inheritance, the same complex suites of enzymes and other proteins – on levels of utterly extraordinary complexity. Our human complexity on this level is of the same order as every other creature. But it's not just that our DNA is similar to everything else that lives. More profound is the truth that our human genome is but one haunting, dominant chord in one melody of the symphony of life, to whose One Total Harmony we are utterly attuned, having been born of it.

Ultimately then, you and I are brother and sister, in rough order of decreasing affinity, with other vertebrates, insects and worms and snails (and slugs), plants and fungi, protists, microbes. Science, in its modern sophistication, is able to give us even the degree of genetic affinity. Only 22% of vertebrate genes are not found in worms or flies; 60% of our genes are shared with rodents, 40% with insects, 40% with nematodes; we share one-third of our genes with plants. We are only 1% different from chimps genetically. 223 of our genes were acquired directly from bacteria. DNA composes in our genomes an ancient, ancient language of which we are learning early and halting words.

This is as scientifically certain as is our new view of the universe, so stunningly visualised for us in the spectacular images beamed home to us by the Hubble telescope. It is as certain as the scientific theory that underlies the machines and gadgets in which we place our absolute everyday confidence. We cannot choose to reject it simply because it threatens our religious viewpoint, or because we think of it as an affront to our dignity – or because of a reluctance to accept we are 'mere animals'.

For those of us who profess to be religious, to think otherwise would be to belittle creation, and thereby its creator: it would make Jobs of us: it is instructive in the light of all this to recall the eponymous hero of the book of that name in the Old Testament who wasn't given the place he felt he deserved in the scheme of things, and argued this endlessly and theologically, never short of words. And then God appears and says (in effect!) 'Who do you think you are?' (see page 90)

If this is how creation works, we need to re-evaluate our notion of God, and the theology which professes to study it scientifically, that it may harmonise in a more mature and intellectually adequate way with the picture revealed to us through cosmology and biology.

The creation-evolution debate

Science can purify religion from error and superstition; religion can purify science from idolatry and false absolutes. Each can draw the other into a wider world, a world in which both can flourish.

Pope John Paul II[13]

In spite of the overwhelming evidence in its favour, many religious people refuse to accept the idea of evolution and a common ancestry for all life. Theodosius Dobzhansky summarised the reasons in a manifesto he published in 1973 as part of the continuing debate over the teaching of evolution in schools in the United States:

Evolution as a process that has always gone on in the history of the earth can be doubted only by those who are ignorant of the evidence or are resistant to evidence, owing to emotional blocks or to plain bigotry.[14]

This refusal is due to the conviction that evolution appears to contradict the account of creation given in scripture and, on a more fundamental level, because it appears to deny the role of God in the process. But there are two books of revelation, as Sir Thomas Browne wrote in the sixteenth century:

... two Books from whence I collect my Divinity; besides that written one of God, another of His servant Nature, that universal and publick Manuscript, that lies expans'd unto the Eyes of all: those that never saw Him in the one have discover'd Him in the other. This was the Scripture and Theology of the Heathens: the natural motion of the Sun made them more admire Him than its supernatural station did the Children of Israel; the ordinary effects of Nature wrought more admiration in them than in the other all his Miracles. Surely the Heathens knew better how to joyn and read these mystical Letters than we Christians, who cast a more careless Eye on these common Hieroglyphicks and disdain to suck Divinity from the flowers of Nature.[15]

These two books cover the same ground. If we are reading the Book of Nature correctly – and all the evidence says that we are – we must conclude that any apparent contradiction suggests we are misinterpreting what is being said to us in scripture. The scriptures are not text-books of science or history. They were not written as such and are not meant to be read as such:

> The Bible itself speaks to us of the origin of the universe and its make-up, not in order to provide us with a scientific treatise but in order to state the correct relationships of man with God and with the universe. Any other teaching about the origin and make-up of the universe is alien to the intentions of the Bible, which does not wish to tell us how the heavens were made but how one goes to heaven.[16]

The attitude of the mainstream churches is very different from what is was even a few decades ago. There is no longer any essential conflict between science and religion on the issue, with the major exception of Islam. The creationist-evolution 'debate' is not, although it may appear as such on the surface, a conflict of science and religion, because the creationist interpretation of the Bible is a false interpretation that needs to be rejected not only on historical grounds, but for moral and religious reasons:

> The central objections to fundamentalist literalism are religious, moral and historical ones. If they are right, this is a case where 'religion' does not clash with science unless something has gone wrong with it already on its own terms. The religion which does clash with science has left its own sphere, for bad reasons, to intrude on a scientific one. It is bad religion.[17]

The mainstream Christian churches have finally embraced evolution and the enrichment that science in general brings to our human understanding of creation:

> What is critically important is that each discipline should

continue to enrich, nourish and challenge the other to be more fully what it can be and contribute to our vision of who we are and who we are becoming.[18]

Creationists of a more fundamentalist persuasion interpret the account of creation in the Book of Genesis more or less literally. A more sophisticated development accepts the evolutionary process, but insists that the evidence of design that pervades the living world requires the direct intervention of God at critical points: otherwise there is no reasonable explanation as to how such complex structures as the eye could evolve. This can be a very compelling argument, especially with regard to the apparently 'irreducible complexity' of biochemical processes.

What Creationism and Intelligent Design have in common is their belief in a creator. For proponents of Intelligent Design this is a creator who intervenes at critical points in evolution to bring about results of such complexity that they could not have been achieved otherwise. This argument from 'irreducible complexity' is a more sophisticated version of the famous watch on the seashore argument of William Paley (page 61). This viewpoint is considered (even in American courts) to be a form of religious belief that cannot be demonstrated scientifically. It cannot be derived from the norms of science. In other words, our scientific description of the creation doesn't need this extra outside dimension for its coherence. Extreme proponents of atheistic science, like Dawkins and Coyne, on the one side, and Michael Behe (who introduced the concept of irreducible complexity) on the other, appear to be poles apart, irreconcilably different.

But there is another alternative, which sees God's hand invisibly acting through the evolutionary process, undetectable as such by scientific intervention. In this perspective the creative potency inherent in the structure of matter replaces the series of discrete creative acts of God demanded by creationist 'science.' The demand that such acts be interventionist and if necessary miraculous, i.e. that God be outside and able to intervene (perhaps miraculously) is inappropriate, partly because at this level of reality any distinction between outside and inside is meaningless.

> In crossing a heath, suppose I pitched my foot against a stone, and were asked how the stone came to be there: I might possibly answer, that for any thing I know to the contrary, it had lain there for ever: nor would it perhaps be very easy to show the absurdity of this answer. But suppose I had found a watch upon the ground, and it should be inquired how the watch happened to be in that place; I should hardly think of the answer which I had before given – that for any thing I knew, the watch might have always been there. Yet why should not this answer serve for the watch, as well as for the stone? why is it not as admissable in the second case as in the first? For this reason, and for no other, viz. that when we come to inspect the watch, we perceive (what we could not discover in the stone) that its several parts are framed and put together for a purpose ... This mechanism being observed ... the inference, we think, is inevitable, that the watch must have had a maker; that there must have existed, at some time, and at some place or other, an artificer or artificers, who formed it for the purpose which we find it actually to answer; who comprehended its construction, and designed its use. For every indication of contrivance, every manifestation of design, which existed in the watch, there exists in the works of Nature ... there is precisely the same proof that the eye was [created] for vision.
>
> William Paley, *Natural Theology*

Of the alternative explanations before us, the one that accords best with the principle of Ockham's Razor, which tells us we must always look for the simplest explanation and 'not multiply entities beyond necessity', would appear to be the last.[19] Special creation and intelligent design require additional buttressing to support the integrity of their intellectual constructs, whereas the notion of a universe without ultimate purpose or meaning fails bewilderingly to accord with the way in which what has unfolded through evolution in human consciousness is tuned to an intelligible universe into which the possibility of intelligence has been programmed. Much more simple and elegant is the notion that intelligence and meaning are utterly inherent. The scientists who study the patterns and relationships that are embedded in the mathematical foundations of all that is, have great faith in their intuitive sense that a correct solution is distinguished by its elegance. God is the simplest and most elegant solution to the equation of the universe. What that simplicity implies, however, is far from simple.

The potential for order and beauty, and ever-growing complexity and awareness, are demonstrably built into the structure of matter at its deepest, most fundamental level. Thus natural selection for complexity is at work not merely in organic evolution, but in the entire course of cosmic development, a direction built ineluctably into the fabric of the universe.[20] Although the ultimate question is whether this requires an outside 'designer' we call God, words such as 'outside/inside' of course make no sense here. The important thing is that what has emerged in our human consciousness is tuned to what is at work in the unfolding of the cosmos. That would be the ultimate wellspring of what we might be able to call a *faith*; leave aside for a moment what it might imply for human perspective, behaviour and destiny. Because if it is true, we may hope that in the end of things all will be well, whatever that means – and we cannot expect to understand what that might mean in any sense.

The diversity of life

Aristotle compiled the first catalogue of biodiversity in the fourth century BC,[21] and the first great compendium of biological diversity in medieval Europe was compiled by Albert the Great (1207-1280).[22] Aristotle and Albert were entirely dependent on direct observation, or the report of (supposedly) direct observation by human eyes; but with the invention of the microscope in the seventeenth century we acquired new eyes (Robert Hookes's *Micrographia* appeared in 1665), enabling us to see and appreciate for the first time the wonder of little lives. Yet, even in John Ray's time (1627-1705), 10,000 seemed an upper limit for the number of invertebrate species.

Our awareness of the vastness of life's diversity grew by orders of magnitude *firstly* with the invention of the microscope, which expanded our horizon upon life in much the same way the invention of the telescope expanded our horizon on the universe; *secondly*, with the great voyages of exploration which brought a first glimpse of biological diversity in other regions of the world – and especially in the tropics, where it is at its greatest. Whereas there are only (!) 20,000 species of insects and spiders in the whole of Great Britain and Ireland, there might be something like 60,000 species in 2 hectares of Ecuadorian rain forest – and as many again 100km away. Edward Wilson once described a single tree in the Tambopata Reserve in Peru that had 43 species of ants belonging to 26 genera, equal to the entire ant fauna of the British Isles. Peter Ashton counted 700 species of trees in 10 selected 1-hectare plots in Borneo – equal in number to the whole tree fauna of North America.[23]

Imposing some kind of order upon such mesmerising diversity presented biologists with a challenging task. The binomial system of classification we use today has a long history, culminating in the work of John Ray and Carl von Linné (Linnaeus).[24]

This system provided a framework that enabled us to envision and describe the relationship between all the different forms of life and, when eventually it became sufficiently three-dimensional, enabled us to see that the pattern is that of a tree springing from one original Acorn of Life (see above, page 56).

Linnaeus

The naming of species
The search for order and system among the bewildering variety of plants, animals and other creatures on earth has exercised people's minds from the earliest days, but the system we use today originated with Linnaeus (1707-1778). The living world is divided into a number of kingdoms. In the system most generally accepted until recently, there are five kingdoms: *Bacteria, Protoctists* (protozoa and slime moulds, various groups of algae and various other unfamiliar aquatic and parasitic organisms), *Animals, Fungi* and *Plants.* Each kingdom comprises a number of *phyla* (singular *phylum*): 12 in the plant kingdom for example, and around 38 in the animal kingdom. Each phylum is subdi-

vided into *classes*, these in turn into a number of *orders*, and the orders in their turn into *families*, each of which contains one or several *genera* (singular *genus*). Each genus comprises a number of different *species* (or just one, in many cases). Each species is given a specific name that consists of two Latin words. The first is the name of the genus (the generic name) which all the species in that genus share, and the second is its own unique, *specific epithet*. Each level in this taxonomic hierarchy constitutes a *taxon*, and as the higher *taxa* are broken down into progressively more numerous lower taxa the organisms in that taxon are increasingly similar and more closely related. Traditionally the organisation of species and genera into higher groupings was done on the basis of visible similarity: of form (morphology), physiology, biochemistry etc, but now we can bring the science of genetics to bear, and while this shows some surprising and hitherto unsuspected relationships, it broadly corroborates the system now in use for two and a half centuries or more.[25]

As we have acquired techniques to study the smallest living entities more adequately, we have come to recognise that there are actually three *domains* of fundamentally different life-forms. What had hitherto been considered as a somewhat obscure group of bacteria characteristic of extreme environments turns out to be a distinct domain of life (the archaea), as different from other bacteria as the latter are from the rest of life. It is now believed that these archaea are among the most abundant groups of organisms on earth.[26] Bacteria and archaea are grouped together as *procaryotes*, distinguished from all other living things (the *eucaryotes*) by the absence of a nucleus and distinct cellular organelles such as mitochondria.[27]

The number of different species of plants, animals and other living things alive on earth today is somewhere between 1.6 and 30 million. The number that have actually been formally described and named is 1.6 million, of which 750,000 species are insects, 250,000 are plants and 41,000 are vertebrates. This, however, is believed to be a mere fraction of the real figure. For example, although the number of described arachnid species is only 75,000, and the number of described roundworm species is somewhere between 15 and 80,000, many researchers believe that the actual number of species in each of these groups is close to a million, allowing both groups to easily surpass the number of described insect species. Terry Erwin and Nigel Stork – foremost authorities in these matters – believe that there may actually be as many as 10 to 80 million arthropod species on the planet.[28]

Linnaeus composed a marvellous metaphor to represent biodiversity. He envisioned it as an enormous mansion with countless corridors and rooms, each the home of a particular group of plants or animals:

> The museum of nature, like a palace, has an enormous number of connected chambers, filled with the stupendous contrivances and wonders of the Creator, to each of which a place is assigned according to its kind; to the greatest amphitheatres of nature the first entry is open to every one, but the smaller ones are usually shut; here there is need of skill to unclose by slow degrees the doorway of each chamber, within which a new world, as it were, displays itself before our eyes … The chief key for unfastening the bars of this palace that has been for all the ages closed is afforded by the microscope, which gives us the same help in examining minute bodies that are close to us as astronomers get from the telescope in the investigation of distant bodies in the heavens.[29]

That figure of up to 30 million species quoted earlier excludes bacteria, whose genetic diversity we have begun to appreciate more fully in recent years. A single spoon of soil from your garden contains 10 trillion bacteria representing as many as 10,000 different species. These immeasurably diverse microscopic creatures are the governors of the worlds their more visible distant cousins bestride like colossi.[30] No group of living things is more ubiquitous or pervasive, or influences our living on so many levels. Indeed, life would not be possible without them. We know so little about them simply because they are so small, and it is only in recent decades that techniques have become available which enable us to get a clearer picture of their complexity, and more recently still of their diversity. It now appears likely that the genetic diversity of bacteria surpasses that of all other living things together: 'The diversity of these micro-organisms dwarfs that of the macroscopic world. Indeed, micro-organisms dominate the tree of life with more than a dozen groups as different from one another as humans are from pine trees.'[31] Bacteria, archaea and unicellular eucaryotes account for at least 90 per cent of living species. It is now generally accepted that the eucaryotic cells of plants and animals arose originally through the fusion of two procaryotic cells: one bacterial and the other archaeal.[32]

It is only now beginning to dawn on us what a critical part viruses play in the evolution and diversity of life. They are the most abundant and diverse genetic entities on earth, outnumbering all other life forms added together. There are perhaps ten million 'types' of viruses, and between them they have a more varied biochemistry than cellular life. The creative power of viruses is now thought to lie behind many early leaps in biomolecular complexity: in other words, they played a defining role in the evolution of key biochemical steps in the development of life. Notice we have to say 'types' rather than species, because of the prevalence in the viral world (virosphere) of *horizontal* gene transfer (HGT), and the fact that they do not reproduce on their own, as cellular organisms do.[33] At least 8% of the human genome is of viral origin, and the percentage could be as high as 50% or more; 35 viral genes appear to play a vital role in human biology.

Although the evolution of life over time is graphically represented by a 'tree of life,' with the blueprint of the species being passed on from one generation to the next by the processes of heredity, we have begun to realise in recent years that the process of HGT is perhaps of equal importance in bacteria and other single-celled organisms – and indeed plays an important role in multicellular organisms like ourselves.[34] For bacteria and archaea the tree of life is more like a web.

The functions of nature

The haemorraging of biological diversity on earth today, mainly as a result of the impact of the burgeoning human population on shrinking natural habitats, is one of the greatest environmental challenges we face: in the first place and most obviously because of the absolute dependence of our human welfare upon it. The most familiar functions the natural world serves in our lives are production and regulation functions: the provision of material goods – food and water, timber and fibres, minerals and so on;

and the regulation of the physical and chemical balances needed for the maintenance of earth's green mantle and the animal and microbial worlds it sustains. But in addition to these, the natural world serves a host of functions of other kinds: less tangible or measurable perhaps because they relate to our interior life. Most familiarly there is the aesthetic appeal of nature, which is rooted in our response to the harmony and beauty of the natural world. The positive effect of experience of nature on our state of mind is something similar, and where that experience permits a deeper encounter with particular creatures – and this can be anything from flowers to elephants – it can transform our perspective on life entirely – a reality acknowledged in the literature on this subject by the recognition of a transformative function of nature.[35]

Why are we so profoundly affected by the experience of nature? Because this is where we really belong. We wear this golden crown of self-awareness, with the capacity for reason, and in this sense we can think of ourselves as being special among the myriads of other species with which we share the planet: but it sits on the head of an animal whose close cousins still swing among the trees of the African savannah. We too were born in the savannah. In this patchwork landscape of open grassland and broken forest of East Africa, separated by the Rift Valley from the dense forests to the west – the Rift Valley itself a mosaic of varied habitats ranging from hot desert to cool upland plateaux – in this open habitat the earliest humans evolved from ancestral apes about 5 million years ago, and by 3 million years had developed several species.

Our distinctive human physique is attuned to this particular natural world of our origins, which is almost literally an extension of our physical being. The flicker of a wild animal against a line of trees at the edge of the forest is an extension of the line of our eyes; the messages in the chorus of birds an extension of our ears, for our eyes and ears have been shaped by a precise evolution to respond to these things, attuning us ever more closely to them. Our feet are made for the touch of grass and the earth, our hands for its feel, our nose to smell this precise world. Just as surely as we are physically shaped for this world of nature, so too are we psychically made for it, and this symbiosis of nature and the human psyche is genetically coded as surely as our colour vision and the shape of our hands and face. It is not something we can shake off, a skin we have outgrown, but built into our genes over the millions of years during which our humanity evolved.[36]

A few tens of thousands of years ago we moved out of Africa, to slowly conquer the world. But we also took Africa with us, because wherever possible we have shaped the natural landscapes we made our own to resemble those in which our minds as our bodies are most at home. For a long time fire, the axe and the goat were the tools with which we shaped nature to our way, then the plough. But all through our long prehistory and history, nature was always on our doorstep: no longer it is true the untamed wilderness, but the experience of trees and flowers, birds and wind and stars, rocks and the sight and sound of rivers and the sea – which satisfied our deep psychological need. The places where nature still breathes awaken in us memories of a deeper childhood. The flowers and trees in every hedgerow awaken them, the singing of the birds, every rock outcrop shaped by time and the elements, every stream that follows the form of the land.

Many people live in a prison of deprivation they don't recognise as a prison, because they have been born in it. The experience of woods carpeted with wood anemones and bluebells should be part of the birthright of every child – the opportunity to catch for a moment an echo of the magic and wonder of the woods of that deeper childhood. We don't know enough about our nature as humans to be able to measure or judge the deeper psychological and spiritual effects of its loss.

This concept – the idea that our need to be out there has its roots as deep as that, that we are more at ease with our lives, healthier, happier in a natural world – is the foundation of the modern Biophilia Hypothesis, on which there is a growing literature of analysis, though an awareness of it runs right through the writings of many thoughtful earlier explorers of nature and landscape.[37] It gives a new depth to our understanding of the functions of the natural world in our lives, and has had a profound influence on professional thinking and practice with regard to its management.

Our mind and spirit, as our body, are most at home in the traditional agricultural landscape which is the cultural counterpart of the open natural landscapes of our origins, endlessly varied in response to different geographies and climates, and to the different traditions into which mankind developed in a new process of cultural adaptive radiation. This traditional rural landscape was our paradise. Always slowly changing and evolving, for landscape is never still, but changing at a pace that allowed the balance to be maintained. Just as is the case with the broader cultural tradition, which may well drown in the flood of resources imported from more aggressive economies, because the continuity of tradition requires change to be slow, allowing adjustment at a pace commensurate with human psychology and the pulse of human generations. Cultural tradition of course is not against change – change is an essential part of it – but it must be change at an evolutionary pace. Material eutrophication often leads to cultural extinction, because it's too much too soon – or, more often than not, too much anyway.[38]

The concept of biophilia, then, accounts to a considerable extent for the profound affect that experience of the natural world has upon us. This is why 'the cry of the wild bird pierces us to the heart; we have never heard that cry before, and it is more familiar to us than our mother's voice.'[39] But that experience of the natural world is increasingly hard to find in our everyday life, which is increasingly drained of its essential characteristics of diversity and quality. Fewer and fewer are the places in the world in which our ordinary days are lived where wild species and natural processes predominate. It is almost impossible to find a place close to where we live and work in which the orchestra of natural sound is not intruded upon – and often drowned out entirely – by the cacophony of our human busyness. It is increasingly difficult to stand under the sky after dark and be awed by the starlight that has bathed the human night since our first glimpse of it, until our conquest of light conquered the dark and we can no longer listen for 'the hidden Things of Darkness' in which God reveals himself.[40]

'In wilderness is the preservation of the world,' wrote Thoreau,[41] and perhaps the concept of biophilia provides us with some of the biological and psychological grounds for such a claim. But it may also be true in a deeper sense. In many cultures there is a spiritual dimension to the experience of nature, which reflects our sense that there is a deeper meaning here, that something more is being said to us here: and this marks the beginning of our attempt not merely to respond to nature, but to understand what that something is: to find words for the way 'things unknown have a secret influence on the soul, and like the centre of the earth violently attract it.'[42]

The remnants of the wild in our midst are not merely cosmetic fringes to the frenetic man-made world. They are the remnants of paradise, through which the face of God in his living revelation to us is glimpsed. The heedless or thoughtless destruction of nature is profanity. Most destruction of the wild is less than deliberate, unaware of the scale of the loss, the value of what is being lost, often to serve the need of the urgent moment. To change this, the momentum of a real, modern, missionary effort is called for, in the true evangelistic sense.[43]

It is against this *theological* background that the catastrophic extinction of life-forms that is occurring today must be evaluated. This extinction seldom results from a deliberate extirpation of species. It is the pressure on the natural world of our growing numbers, coupled with the expectation of constant growth and ever-higher 'living standards' that is responsible. In our lifetime the human population has doubled or even trebled, from 3 billion in 1960 to 6.8 billion today. The effects of this on the atmosphere, on the waters of land and sea and on natural ecosystems are unsustainable – beyond earth's capacity to renew or resolve or heal on human time-scales. As the area available for them to live their free lives diminishes under the advancing tide of humanity, as many as a quarter of the world's mammals are in danger of extinction by 2030. Lion populations have fallen by nearly 90% in the past 20 years. Tigers are on the verge of becoming extinct in the wild; gorillas and chimpanzees are in grave danger of doing likewise. No fewer than 90% of the larger fishes have disappeared from the oceans in the last 50 years. At least 1 in 8 known plant species is threatened with extinction: to say nothing of the innumerable invertebrate species of whose plight we know least, but which account for the overwhelmingly greater portion of the diversity of life on earth. If present trends continue – and there are few signs to the contrary – 20% of all species of plants and animals could be extinct within 30 years, and half of all species by the end of this century.[44]

Human population growth					2050	10 billion
				2000	6 billion	
			1986	5 billion		
		1975	4 billion			
	1960	3 billion				
1927	2 billion					
1825	1 billion					

Palaeobiodiversity: vanished forms most wonderful

No creature but one like unto Holy Angels can see into all ages. Sure this power was not given in vain, but for some wonderful purpose; worthy of itself to enjoy and fathom.

Traherne, *Centuries of Meditations* I, 55

Do we not know that in the evolution of species a century is but as a drop of rain that is caught in the swirl of the river, and that millenaries glide as swiftly over the life of universal matter as single years over the history of a people?

Maeterlinck's *The Life of the Bee*

None of our fellow mortals is safe who eats what we eat, who in any way interferes with our pleasures, or who may be used for work or food, clothing or ornament, or mere cruel, sportish amusement. Fortunately many are too small to be seen, and therefore enjoy life beyond our reach. And in looking through God's great stone books made up of records reaching back millions and millions of years, it is a great comfort to learn that vast multitudes of creatures, great and small and infinite in number, lived and had a good time in God's love before man was created.

John Muir, *Boyhood*, page 39

It may be argued that there is nothing new about this loss of biodiversity. Is it not part of the natural order of evolution? During any period of geological time we care to visit we find a level of biodiversity comparable to what we find today, but in each epoch different from ours, each a unique section across the progress of organic evolution. Species come and go over geological time: the fossil record is thought to represent perhaps one in every 20,000 species that have existed.[45] During the past 250 million years there have been episodes of extinction at intervals of 26 million years.[46] The greatest of these, which occurred at the end of the Permian period of geological time, appears to have been caused by changes in the configuration of the earth's landmasses, especially the conglomeration of all the continents into a single mass called Pangaea. With the concomitant loss of a great deal of seashore, climate change, and new volcanic activity, 54% of the families of marine invertebrates went extinct over a 5- to 8-million year period (as did an even higher proportion of genera and species).

By geological standards, the mass extinction that occurred at the end of the Permian was rapid, but it took more than a thousand times as long to occur as the much smaller but virtually instantaneous 3000-year extinction of the large land mammals of North America. The four other mass extinction events each saw the loss of 15% to 22% of the marine invertebrate families extant at the time, although none compare with the end-Permian event. The dramatic mass extinction that occurred at the end of the Cretaceous period is thought to have been triggered by the impact of a small asteroid that crashed into the earth in the Gulf of Mexico. The train of consequences it caused saw the disappearance of the dinosaurs from land and ammonites from the seas, and brought an end to the era of 'middle-life' on earth. Tetrapods were affected far more than fish or invertebrates; of the 89 taxonomic families of tetrapods then extant, 36 were lost: i.e. it had more of a dry land impact – plants and tetrapods were worst hit. Plants generally do not suffer mass extinction events as drastic as the various animal groups, but on this occasion perhaps 75% of the extant plant species perished.[47]

What is different about the Sixth Extinction that is taking place today is that it is occurring at a rate that is 1,000 to 10,000 times greater than the natural rate, and is not due to some concatenation of natural events as were all previous mass extinctions. It is caused by a failure of intelligence and virtue on the part of the only rational species on the planet: failure to control our population; abuse of earth's resources and environmental support systems to maintain the profligate and unsustainable living of an affluent minority, a way of living to which the rest aspire; our failure to appreciate the deeper worth of the natural world and, most radically, the loss of faith in an ultimate meaning that might encourage us to believe and behave differently.

Whether we are religious or not, whether we feel the need of a dimension of meaning beyond the mechanical explanation or not, we cannot but see the march of evolution as a glorious pageant, a progression of 'endless forms most beautiful and most wonderful'.[48] But for the believer it raises a further question. The human story is part of the pageant of life but not a necessary part of it. It opens a new act in the drama, a new level of possibility, yet on a re-run of evolution it might all have turned out differently, without human eyes and minds to appreciate it all.[49] And in any case, for all of evolutionary time until the blink of an eye ago there were no human onlookers to wonder and appreciate.

Eight centuries before Thomas, St Augustine could still intuit the inherent worth of all creatures, in an age when little was known of the real diversity of life and nothing of evolution, and the way in which each in its way is a unique expression of What God Is:

> It is not with respect to our convenience or discomfort, but with respect to their own nature, that the creatures are glorifying to their Artificer.[50] How admirable these things are in their own places, how excellent in their own natures, how beautifully adjusted to the rest of creation, and how much grace they contribute to the universe by their own contributions as to a commonwealth.[51]

The pleasure we derive from observation and contemplation of the natural world, because we are endowed with the capacity to think the way we do, is a faint echo of the self-fulfillment God achieves through creation. Past and present, these endless forms most beautiful and most wonderful, each one unique, are different expressions of life's potential, each made with the same loving care as we are: which charges us with the obligation to bestow on them *a measure of consideration commensurate with that role*. We need to profoundly re-assess our ethical stance with regard to the family of life on earth in the light of this new perspective (see page 93).

This last is especially significant when we are asking questions about the purpose of creation, because there was no human eye to see and admire in these earlier ages, no human mind to seek an explanation. Only in the last few minutes of life's journey through time has a consciousness capable of reflecting and asking these questions appeared. This profoundly significant thought reinforces the argument of Thomas Aquinas that created nature is not intended primarily for us: it is for God's own pleasure. What this suggests is that this extinct creation was not primarily intended for our admiration: this is not its primary purpose. From a theological perspective, the mesmeric diversity of life in the past, kaleidoscopically evolving over time, has the same *ultimate* purpose as does contemporary biodiversity, so succinctly summarised all of 750 years ago by Aquinas: 'God cannot express himself fully in any one creature: and so he has produced many and diverse life forms, so that what one lacks in its expression of divine goodness may be compensated for by others: for goodness, which in God is single and undifferentiated, in creatures is refracted into a myriad hues of being.'[52]

The Franciscan Bonaventure wrote about creation at around the same time as Thomas (they died the same year).[53] But for Bonaventure 'all the creatures of this sensible world … are the shadows, echoes and pictures, the vestiges, images and manifestations of that most powerful, most wise and best first principle … They are set before us for the sake of our knowing God, and are divinely given signs. For every creature is by its very nature a kind of portrayal and likeness of that eternal Wisdom.' This is Neo-Platonism. In other words, for Bonaventure creatures are mere signposts that point in the direction of God, but for Thomas they are *incarnations of the divine*.[54]

And at this point we must pause to observe the way in all this discussion we use the word 'God', 'God's pleasure', which are words that easily fitted into the earlier geocentric, homocentric worldview; but we have to rethink our concepts of what they might intend in the light of all that science has revealed about the nature of creation. They need to evolve and mature if they are to function meaningfully in the changed context of this new worldview.

If we profess a religious view of things, we can no longer be in doubt that the self-expression of the Divine in the living world of which St Thomas speaks did not begin when human words appeared on the earth to write and talk and sing about it: the symphony has been unfolding since the beginning. We can see the kernel of this view of creation in the preoccupation of early Islamic and Christian philosophy with creation as word.

There is no questioning the fact that we are all made with the same exquisite care, that we all share the same extraordinarily complex chemistry, the scorpion and the daisy and the worm no less than our human selves. The most marvellous achievement of modern genetics has been to show in ever-greater detail the nature and extent of that relationship. I have the same kind of genetic make-up, often the very same genes, as the scorpion and the daisy and the worm.

'A myriad hues of being': the dignity of the individual species

The consideration of these appearances might induce us to be-lieve that variety itself, distinct from every other reason, was a motive in the mind of the Creator, or with the agents of his will.
William Paley, *Natural Theology* (1802), Chapter XIX

Each of his creatures is incomprehensible to us also, in the sense that no one has a perfect understanding but he. We recognise and appropriate aspects of them, and logic is useful in register-ing these aspects and what they might imply; but it does not give us to know even one individual being.
John Henry Newman, *Grammar of Assent*

The diversity of the living creation is more wonderful, admirable, complex by orders of magnitude than we once imagined, or could have imagined – and yet not beyond comprehension, be-cause the most extraordinary thing is that we can understand it. To recall Einstein's phrase, 'The eternal mystery of the world is its comprehensibility.'

But there is a real danger that in discussing biodiversity we lose sight of the moral immensity of its diminution at our hands. Species are not reducible to numbers. The variety of life is not that of a great stamp collection, with stamps of ever nation, every shape and colour, every period and value, every mode of philatelic expression. Each species in this catalogue of life is the unique living embodiment of an evolutionary journey as long as our own, a journey that has a common starting point with ours, and like ours is an ongoing journey.[55] Its extinction is the loss of a unique mode of life's possibility, each in its way an achieve-ment as great as ours, a 'unique contribution to the common-wealth'. No species on earth has undergone, through all of our universe's time, its marvelous becoming just to be snuffed out of existence at our whim or through our pursuit of shallow, trivial ends. Its time will come in the course of life and the earth's revolutions, but that is not ours to call or foreshorten. If you speak the language of belief in God, and embrace what the revelation of science tells you, then no species is insignificant. Each is worthy in the eyes of God, deserving of our respect and study and admiration. Even, and perhaps especially, the most obscure. 'For heaven God has created the angels,' wrote Saint Augustine, 'and for the earth creatures that crawl, and neither is superior to the other: because the hand of man can no more create a worm than an angel.'[56]

And there is another side to this. Species are the etymology of creation; understanding, appreciating them, deepens our appreciation of the language God uses. The loss of any species is the loss of one colour more from the rainbow of life's diversity. This is exegesis on a deeper, more fundamental and universal level than dissecting the language of scriptures with their layers of human fallibility. This understanding of creation needs to shape the syntax of theology, not the other way around. And doing this will break the mould in which we confine the infinite God, keeping him or her to a size we are comfortable with. God's comfort may not be ours, shaped as ours is by the physical that is dominant in our being.[57]

Among the elephants
Although the reality of other species is utterly independent of us, and they 'exist in totally different worlds,' the world of our experience can interact with theirs, and be enriched through that contact as by no other experience on earth.

When I was living in Malawi once upon a time, I spent a few days on my own on one occasion at a small game camp near a mission station in Lwangwa, on the west wide of the Zambezi river. The camp was maybe six or seven fairly small tents in a large clearing in the bush. And one night there, I was awakened by a sort of whispering sound, so I went out to see what it might be and walked into the clearing away from my tent – it was a bright night, with a moon. And suddenly, out of nowhere, the whispering surrounded me, and it was the sound of elephants passing by, walking among the tents, on their way somewhere about their own business – 'as if they had an appointment at the end of the world'[58] – carefully stepping in that extraordinarily deliberate and silent way they have with their great feet, yards from where I stood transfixed, quite unheeding of my insignificant presence. Transfixed is the word for it, the hair on the back of my head on end, not out of fear but in awe of this thing that was happening, at the sheer wonder of their presence in the night, at such grace surrounding me. And in two minutes I suppose they were gone, and the world was empty.

All my reading and all my study of science had not prepared me for the reality of encounter with this creature. The other thing I remember was a new sense of the way we humans bestride the narrow world like colossi, in Shakespeare's phrase. How can anybody who experiences this presence be so presumptuous as to deny this creature its God-given place on the earth? How can anyone who has been face to face with the elephant butcher it frivolously – so that some of us may use its teeth to decorate ourselves or its feet as umbrella stands in fashionable hallways – or banish it from the home for which it is made, so that we can grow more tobacco?

Is that why we are given this tiny spark of God's own creativeness, so that we can use it to diminish the diversity of the creation? Is it not rather given us primarily in order to understand who and what we are, what our place in the creation is? If there is a deeper meaning to the naming of the animals in Genesis, as God leads them all before Adam, it is surely the injunction to come to know them and to understand them, for they have come from his hand with precisely the same loving care as we have. God cares about them as much as he cares about us, if differently. The more deeply we grow in our understanding of the creation through the best exercise of that divine spark of intelligence that is in us, the more deeply we understand that reality, and the extraordinary closeness of our kinship with them.

Francis of Assisi could talk of Brother Wolf and we approve the metaphor. But we now know it is not a metaphor. We are brother and sister, elephant and wolf and man and woman, oak and dandelion, frog and dragonfly. To think we are more is to diminish God, to imagine they are less is to diminish ourselves. We can not think otherwise once we bring our intellect and spirit

to bear on the physical reality of the diverse living species of creation, all these manifestations of the kaleidoscope of the creativity of the Great Being 'in whom all potentialities already exist as
a plan of action,'[59] the contemplation of which so thrilled
Thomas Aquinas (see above, page 74). If we see them in any lesser way than the unique mind and spirit God has given us enables us to see and understand them – and ourselves – we are
failing in our use of that one supreme talent (in the sense of the
talents in Jesus' parable) that our species alone has been given,
and surely there will come a day when an account of the way we
have used it will be required of us.

In the modern scientific paradigm, species are primarily objects to be studied and better understood so that we may make
better use of them. This is often the governing rationale in biodiversity studies and research programmes, and our thinking
outside the laboratory is not all that different. We behave as
though the rest of the species in creation were toys God has
given us to play with. We think we can therefore do with them
as we like, for they are only toys, *simulacra*, even if we emphasise
our responsibility to care for them. Whereas what God has given
us are brothers and sisters brought into being with the same
care, so that we can learn through them of other dimensions of
his being.

We may like to think of ourselves as being a little less than
the angels, but we have been swept along by precisely the same
exhilarating evolutionary maelstrom as all the other species
which people this moment of life's time with us, 4,000 million
years of life having been spent travelling with them, and before
that we have shared the same remote origins in the dust of ex-
ploding stars.

It is not difficult perhaps to see or to accept what I am saying
about the elephant: that the experience, the confrontation of our
spirit with their different spirit, allied to our understanding of
their comparable and at times greater physical and biochemical
complexity, shatters the thin psychological barrier that enables
us to treat them as less than God intends, to take away their dignity as creatures shaped with the same loving care that we are.
But the wonder of the biological achievement of every species
on this earth is comparable to that of the elephant. Not the same,

for each is different, but of the same magnitude and significance.

This realisation underpins a true moral imperative for us. Reverence for life is required of us, and not as an optional extra, to be applied when it suits us or only when it is easy, but as a radical precept, shaping the very roots of human behaviour. In more traditional language it vibrates at the heart of the first of the Ten Commandments, and at the heart of the second commandment. And, come to think of it, at the heart of the third commandment.[60]

Consider the dipper

Consider now the life of the dipper, a bird of fast-flowing rivers and streams, especially in mountains and hills, which walks or dips underwater, remaining submerged to feed on aquatic insects. This is its habitat, the corner of the world for which it has been quite precisely shaped by millions of years of evolution. But the dipper is much more than this. All the time the waterfall is in its ears, an endlessly varying symphony of sound that is different for every part of the river, different at different times of the year, so different that each spot on the river could be identified by the dipper from its distinctive harmony alone. The dipper, in a sense, is the waterfall. Its ears know nothing of any world of sound beyond the water. Its genes and proteins are so attuned to every nuance of the movement and sound of the water and the dance of light and current; it belongs in this place so intimately that every detail is part of its being in a way we can never really appreciate because it is so far beyond our superficial experience of a corner of the world that evolution has endowed the dipper to belong in and respond to with all the biological capacity, but very differently tuned and pitched, that we humans possess. For the dipper, one stretch of stream is its entire world: it experiences no other. It reflects the ecological essence of the stream; it is its spirit. As for its song, 'In a general way his music is that of the streams refined and spiritualised. The deep booming notes of the falls are in it, the trills of rapids, the gurgling of margin eddies, the low whispering of level reaches, and the sweet tinkle of separate drops oozing from the ends of mosses and falling into tranquil pools ... I have often observed him singing in the midst of beaten spray, his music completely buried beneath the water's roar; yet I knew he was surely singing by his gestures and the movements of his bill.'[61]

> It has been here for eons. It has been adapting to this special place of the earth for uncounted millennia. Every hair, every sensilla, is a response to this place which it knows with absolute intimacy. Can such a creature be said to know? It has eyes and ears, different indeed from ours, but in their way and for their purpose sharper perhaps; it sees and hears and in its own way affirms its being. It has a heart and blood and kidneys, different beyond familiarity from our own and sometimes with different names, but doing what our heart and blood and kidneys do. It knows sex as we do in its different way. It is utterly beautiful, which is one reason I return to look at it over and over again. The scientist does not study nature because it is useful. He studies it because he delights in it and he delights in it because it is beautiful.
>
> Jules Henri Poincaré (1845-1912). Quoted in *The Quest for Life in Amber* by George and Roberta Poinar

But the important thing here is to appreciate that the sensory capacity of the animal equips it to respond in a way that is comparable with our own human response. It might have been possible in Descartes' day for some people to think an animal was an elaborate piece of clockwork, that its responses were automatic, that it was incapable of feeling pain or joy, much less anything beyond. But now our science shows us that on a physical level it has everything we have, and if we can take a step far enough back to see the entire picture – to view things holistically – it is so obvious that the very purpose of these capacities is to enable it to respond, to feel: and these feelings will include joy and pain – even if at this moment science finds it difficult to devise calipers of sufficient sensitivity to take hold of it or rulers of a sensitivity adequate to its measurement.

> The structures of the insect's body exhibit a perfection that, from a mechanical point of view, is unsurpassed, while the external beauty of some of the creatures makes them fit associates of the most delicate flowers or no mean rivals of the most gorgeous of the feathered world.
>
> David Sharp, *Cambridge Natural History* Vol 5

And with our theological spectacles on again we might say that by being in this way the dipper acclaims creation. Smaller words hardly do its being justice, because they fail to catch the true significance of its biological closeness to us, or of the possibility that its response might not be so different from the acclaim that is expected of ourselves. Its heart beats like ours, but tuned to the sound of the waterfall; its blood flows like ours but modulated to the swirl of the current. Its brain is a miniature of ours but geared for feather and flight and an appetite for caddis grubs and for a joy that affirms the goodness in the differentness of its experience of the one corner of creation it knows best, better than any other creature. Its spirit and its soul are as ours on this profound level, not in some superficial way, for truly was it created with the same loving care. The role of each and every species is not merely ecological, it is spiritual; it is a unique shout of joy, affirmation, worship that no other species can give. If any species is missing – if the dipper has become extinct say – a note which I cannot replace is missing from the symphony.

I celebrate the dipper above other species in part because it has lived in my spirit for sixty years. It nested under the bridge over the river that flowed beside the house in which I was born, and perhaps its call was part of the song of the river that bore me to sleep as a child (many years before the noise of traffic over the bridge came to drown all the voices of the natural world). The happiest hours of my childhood were spent along the river we shared then, and the affective foundation upon which this book rests was put in place during those years. But over and beyond that I chose the dipper because it is somehow easier to isolate not only its world, but its heartbeat, and touch however faintly, at however great a distance, the fringe of its joy.

Natura in minimis

And size is no measure of complexity. *Natura in minimus maxime miranda*, wrote Linnaeus: it is in the smallest creatures that nature is at its most marvellous. In the smallest indeed may be the greatest wonders, as Sir Thomas Browne – among many others – recognised long ago when he wrote so quaintly in the early part of the 17th century of insects and spiders that 'in these narrow Engines there is more curious Mathematicks; and the civility of these little Citizens more neatly sets forth the Wisdom of their Maker'.[62] 'The universe would be incomplete without man; but it would also be incomplete without the smallest transmicroscopic creature that dwells beyond our conceitful eyes and knowledge.'[63]

> The hinges in the wings of an earwig, and the joints of its antennae, are as highly wrought as if the Creator had nothing else to finish.
>
> William Paley, *Natural Theology*, Chapter XXVII

The emperor penguins

We are very seldom able to observe the life of another species in a way sufficiently detailed and intimate to allow us the beginning of an appreciation of the way each species is at the centre of its own world. A rare instance is that splendid film *March of the Penguins*, which allows us to spend an hour in the company of this one other species, albeit from the comfort of our armchair, well away from the cold and silence of distant Antarctica, but close enough to glimpse the marvel of its evolutionary achievement, especially in terms of its adaptation to the challenge of surviving in this particularly harsh environment.[64] It also allows us to hear the faintest whisper of the interior life of the species. But a comparable film could be made of every single species on earth, if we were privileged to have the leisure and the technical equipment and know-how to make it. You feel the same before beetles and buttercups and ferns when you know them for what they are. Once the light of our prodigious modern understanding is brought to bear on them, especially the light of the microscope, the partitions that separate us shatter, partitions put there by a presumption that makes little Lucifers of us, no less, confused with the idea that because the light of the divinity beyond sparkles faintly in us, we are as God. Those who study a particular group of plants or animals intimately, as professionals or perhaps even more so as amateurs, are afforded glimpses of these other lives over and over again. It affords them a pleasure and a sense of fulfillment no other human activity can give because in doing so we intimate through our contact with these other modes of existence, through our experience of these other possibilities realised through evolution's unfolding, unique expressions of the divine goodness, beauty and terror.

No doubt the new visual techniques that enable us to see and wonder at creatures on the smallest scale in all their splendour for the first time will allow them to enter the living room via our TV and computer screens as the ability of the camera to capture them becomes ever more sophisticated and cheaper. And when they do, as they will, our eyes will be opened in the same way to a wider spectrum of life's glorious and frightening diversity. And it is not only in the jungle and the desert that this wild splendour reflects God's glory. It is on our own doorstep, if we weren't too eternally busy to stop, to look, to see, and then to wonder and praise. There is truly more to wonder at, more to bring us to our knees, than our short lifetimes can ever compass, in the pond, and along the fringe of the bog, and in the last bit of woodland in my local parish.

Exile from nature

Perhaps it was the birth of human consciousness that drove us from the garden of Eden, and we ceased to be able to experience the world as the animal does, without our mind being full at every moment, conscious or unconscious, of thought. Today we can recover that ecstasy of pre-human being which is the animal's experience of the world only at rare moments, when the nature we have abandoned brushes the edge of our newly-awakened consciousness. No-one has written more eloquently of this than William Hudson. When he was a young man, Hudson would ride out across the plains of Patagonia for days on end, away from all human contact, and knew there 'the elation ... the feeling experienced on going back to a mental condition we have outgrown ...'

> For I had undoubtedly gone back; and that state of intense watchfulness, or alertness rather, with suspension of the higher intellectual faculties, represented the mental state of the pure savage. He thinks little, reasons little, having a surer guide in his instinct; he is in perfect harmony with nature, and is nearly on a level, mentally, with the wild

animals he preys on, and which in their turn sometimes prey on him. If the plains of Patagonia affect a person in this way, even in a much less degree than in my case, it is not strange that they impress themselves so vividly on the mind, and remain fresh in memory, and return frequently; while other scenery, however grand or beautiful, fades gradually away, and is at last forgotten. To a slight, in most cases probably a very slight, extent, all natural sights and sounds affect us in the same way; but the effect is often transitory, and is gone with the first shock of pleasure, to be followed in some cases by a profound and mysterious melancholy. The greenness of earth; forest and river and hill; the blue haze and distant horizon; shadows of clouds sweeping over the sun-flushed landscape – to see it all is like returning to a home which is more truly our home than any habitation we know. The cry of the wild bird pierces us to the heart; we have never heart that cry before, and it is more familiar to us than our mother's voice.

And we ourselves are the living sepulchres of a dead past – that past which was ours for so many thousands of years before this life of the present began; its old bones are slumbering in us – dead, and yet not dead nor deaf to nature's voices; the noisy burn, the roar of the waterfall, and thunder of long waves on the shore, and the sound of rain and whispering winds in the multitudinous leaves, bring it a memory of the ancient time; and the bones rejoice and dance in their sepulchre.[65]

Overlain as our mind is with intellect, much of that pure sensory experience of the fullness of creation is denied us or we have denied it to ourselves. But we can recapture it from time to time. And it is this that enables us to touch the edge of the dipper's elation.

The dipper is absorbed in the experience of his reality. The dipper, in being and existence, affirms creation and creator by being what he is, fully in his world. We are privileged to be observers of his life, and through our intellect alone among the creatures on earth, to understand his life history and the history of his kind. What makes our human response different is that our peculiar physical endowment (the nature of our brain in particular) enables us to move a small step beyond the aware response of the dipper into self-awareness and understanding. But that is the extent of our wisdom in this regard. For although this is the one thing which truly sets us apart and can be seen as a talent greater than that given to any other creature, the new capacity with which we are endowed as a result is severely limited.

We cannot reach up to the mind of God to share his knowledge of 'what is going on' up there – any more than it is possible for the dipper to understand what is going on at the level of my understanding. We are simply not equipped biologically to do so. Colin Tudge reminds us (paraphrasing Kant) 'that human beings can understand only what they are equipped to understand … Our brains partake of chemistry, and chemistry is only an aspect of the whole; and, as survival machines, our brains cotton on only to those aspects of the universe that are pertinent to survival. Natural selection has not equipped us to understand in any broad sense.'[66] And if our senses can't go there, words won't go there either.

Our biological capacities have been sharpened by evolution to fit us for a particular niche on the earth. The admiration of an observer from space might largely be concentrated on how beautifully everything about us is adapted for this one niche. But our human understanding takes us beyond that niche, into realms above and beyond anything our hunter-gatherer primate endowment has equipped us to imagine (form an image) – as distinct from conceptualise.

Though it is away beyond the scope of this book, it is tantalising to re-envision the notion of angels in this light: possible levels of apprehension between our limited beginnings of intelligence and the Ultimate. Lucifer, the light-bearer, was such a being, brightest of the angels, and because he was so bright, beyond all creatures beneath him, unable to accept that there could be a level above him. Are we not in danger of the same presumption on our humbler level? Surely reverence must be the dominant note in our affirmation, one octave only above the dipper's acclaim?

The animal as subject

> Sympathy beyond the confines of man is one of the latest moral
> acquisitions.
>
> Charles Darwin, *Descent of Man* (1874)

For all our detailed understanding of how life functions, plant
and other animal species are always somewhere outside us in
the circle of a world at the centre of which we ourselves stand.
We think of ourselves as the only real subject in the world. An
experience like my encounter with the elephants is transformative because it allows us to sense, just for those few minutes,
the way in which this creature is at the centre of the world, as
much the subject about which everything in the ecosystem revolves, as we perceive ourselves to be.

But the realisation is beginning to dawn on the scientific
mind that animals must feel as we do: each in its own species-
specific way, but in the same integrated manner of responding
as a subject in the corner of the ecosystem for which evolution
has shaped it. The animal, mammal or bird or insect or worm, is
from its unique perspective the subject, each at the centre of a
world, and all their worlds overlap and influence each other:
and this is what ecology is all about: in the words of Albert
Schweitzer, ecology is 'the science of the architecture of creation.'
And to be fully what *we* are meant to be, we need to apprehend
the animal as subject, at the centre of its world. But the subject in
species other than our own is hidden within, inaccessible to the
science of our time. If we would see the true picture we need
somehow to be able to reach out to touch that alien mind – the
mind of the other – and relate to it.

The differences that distinguish one species from another
exist to an extent because each species is uniquely adapted to exploit the resources of one particular niche, which is different for
every creature. They are differences of degree rather than kind
when considered in this ecological sense. The ecological niche of
each species is the corner of the world for which it is quite precisely made; physically in ways which evoke in us an ever-
growing wonder the more we understand and decipher this
adaptation; and psychologically, though this operates in what is
still a biologically dark region of which we understand little.

The landscape of an animal other than man is almost literally a physical part of it, an extension of its senses; it is what its senses reach out to and connect, it is what it was made for. For most creatures, *where* they are is *who* they are, so precisely are they made for a specific place. Put them in different surroundings and they are no longer themselves and often cannot survive.

We are making much headway in seeing that the physiology, the biochemistry, the genetics of other than human lives are all on the same level of complexity as ours – on a much higher level in some respects, even if our mode of being is unique by being on the higher level of reflective self-consciousness. We are beginning to acknowledge that animals may feel as we do. All the evidence points in this direction when we confront the animal holistically. Only in the context of the kind of narrow dualism made fashionable by Descartes and his disciples was the distorted interpretation that much of scientific endeavour picked up on made possible, when the mechanical part of the means by which the animal's response comes about is taken to be the whole explanation.[67]

It is perhaps not all that difficult to accept – both emotionally and intellectually – that those animals closest to us on the evolutionary tree experience the same range of emotions we do, each differently and each uniquely, in the manner appropriate to the particular ecological niche it occupies. And to an extent therefore we can share in those emotions. Anyone who has kept a pet or works closely with birds or mammals understands this. But it would be wrong to treat them as juveniles or exotic variants of ourselves.

Human encounters with wild animals provide us with the most striking examples of experiences by means of which the boundary between our world and their world can vanish for a moment. These are often transformative experiences, enabling us to see something to which we were blind before, and which alters forever our attitude to life. There is an extensive literature dealing with experiences such as this, one of the most famous being the encounter with a dying wolf that converted Aldo Leopold into the great apostle of a conservation ethic he went on to become.

> We were eating lunch on a high rimrock, at the foot of which a turbulent river elbowed its way. We saw what we

thought was a doe fording the torrent, her breast awash in white water. When she climbed the bank toward us and shook out her tail, we realised our error: it was a wolf. A half-dozen others, evidently grown pups, sprang from the willows and all joined in a welcoming melee of wagging tails and playful maulings. What was literally a pile of wolves writhed and tumbled in the centre of an open flat at the foot of our rimrock.

In those days we had never heard of passing up a chance to kill a wolf. In a second we were pumping lead into the pack, but with more excitement than accuracy; how to aim a steep downhill shot is always confusing. When our rifles were empty, the old wolf was down, and a pup was dragging a leg into impassable side-rocks.

We reached the old wolf in time to watch a fierce green fire dying in her eyes. I realised then, and have known ever since, that there was something new to me in those eyes – something known only to her and to the mountain. I was young then, and full of trigger-itch; I thought that because fewer wolves meant more deer, that no wolves would mean hunters' paradise. But after seeing the green fire die, I sensed that neither the wolf nor the mountain agreed with such a view.[68]

In his autobiography, John Muir recounts an episode that took place early in life and which had something of the same effect on him. His family had recently emigrated from Scotland, and they had carved a farm out of the Wisconsin woodland. Their sow had given birth to a large litter, which she took into the woods to forage for roots and acorns when they were old enough. On one occasion a wandering Indian shot one of the little pigs, causing the mother and her remaining offspring to hurtle in terror back to the farm shanty for protection.

The solemn awe and fear in the eyes of that old mother and those little pigs I never can forget; it was as unmistakable and deadly a fear as I ever saw expressed by any human eye, and corroborates in no uncertain way the oneness of all of us.[69]

But the further we move away from where we are on the Tree of Life, as we approach modes of existence more remote from ours in evolutionary terms (when for example 'we walk with the lone worm, wandering in the twilight of consciousness'[70]), the more difficult this becomes, because their anatomy and physiology are very different from ours, and because their sensory perceptions, and what emotional responses these generate or facilitate, are often beyond anything we can touch with fellow feeling. Our sympathy and empathy with them, therefore, must go beyond shared emotions to reside in our understanding and the behaviour towards them that understanding dictates. And, of course, 'how little we know as yet of the life of plants – their hopes and fears, pains and enjoyments.'[71]

Nature cannot be experienced other than as it is, and then only by one person; this is simply a reflection of the great defect of modern society – that few can live in any real contact with nature.

In my own firm opinion, nature and the countless ways we have discovered to reproduce it, visually, aurally and verbally, are antipathetic; above all I believe it is so verbally. Words cannot reproduce nature; they exist in totally different worlds.

This is for me one of the great claims of birds: that however familiar and common they are, they cannot really be described. We cannot write of them in our own terms and certainly not in theirs. ... swallows coming in across the sea from France. What did they feel?

John Fowles, *New Scientist* 3 January 2004, p 75

And that behaviour must now, in the light of our new understanding, be governed by an ethical imperative that rests first of all on our appreciation of other species as living self-expressions of God, each species a unique note in that stupendous orchestra, a unique hue in the super-psychedelic rainbow of life; secondly, on our ever-growing understanding of our shared history, our family connections, our common destiny on earth; and thirdly, because we now see so clearly that without them and the biosphere they constitute, our human life is, in proportion to our neglect and abuse of that biological diversity, diminished and ultimately smothered.

The South African poet Roy Campbell, playfully and perhaps with a hint of satirical challenge to our anthropocentric theology, articulates this wonderfully in his synopsis of the theology of Bongwi, the baboon.[72]

> This is the wisdom of the Ape
>   Who yelps beneath the Moon –
> 'Tis God who made me in His shape
>   He is a Great Baboon.
> 'Tis He who tilts the moon askew
>   And fans the forest trees,
> The heavens which are broad and blue
>   Provide him his trapeze;
> He swings with tail divinely bent
>   Around those azure bars
> And munches to his Soul's content
>   The kernels of the stars;
> And when I die, His loving care
>   Will raise me from the sod
> To learn the perfect Mischief there,
>   The Nimbleness of God.

Job and the whale

T.H. Huxley warned of the danger of reading a modern viewpoint into the writings of the ancients: 'There is no snare in which the feet of a modern student of ancient lore are more easily entangled, than that which is spread by the similarity of the language of antiquity to modern modes of expression.'[73] Huxley was referring to the extraordinarily modern-sounding aphorisms of some of the pre-Socratic philosophers, but the same warning is appropriate for our tendency to seek corroboration for our cherished preconceptions in the poetic depths of sacred scripture. Although we need to keep this caveat before us, it may be we can discern earlier intimations of the perspective argued here in God's chapter-long eulogy to Job on the whale (Job 40, 41).

The background to it is this. Job is a good man, one of the best, 'a perfect and an upright man, one that feareth God, and escheweth evil'. And yet, for all his righteousness, God permits every conceivable disaster to befall him. He loses his family and his wealth, and finally he is smitten 'with sore boils from the sole of his foot unto his crown'. Job wants to know how God could allow this to happen to him, acknowledging at the same time that the ways of God are beyond our comprehension, 'for he is not a man, as I am, that I should answer him, and we should come together in judgement'. This goes on for 37 chapters, during which Job bemoans his condition and God's unfairness at length, and the three friends who have come to sit with him make their various less-than-comforting contributions. And then at last, out of the whirlwind, God answers.

How little you know, he seems to say. Your horizons are so narrow and you are only a newcomer on the stage of life. 'Where wast thou when I laid the foundations of the earth ... Hast thou entered into the springs of the sea? Or hast thou walked in search of the depth?' Can you even begin to understand the wonder that is the whale, 'whose eyes are like the eyelids of the morning,' this wondrous mode of being on the earth over whose gestation I watched through eons while you were but a twinkle in my eye? What do you know of the wonder of its intelligent life, its astonishing evolutionary progress from land to sea?[74] Have you the empathy to reach through our kinship and touch the sense of its subjectivity in its world? Can you begin to imagine the fullness of the whale's achievement, the acclaim of its being, the joy of its existence, 'whose like there is not upon earth, who is made without fear ... [who] is a king over all the children of pride'?[75] Just because you are a step closer to God in one or two ways (though many steps further away in others)? Do you consider and ponder all these things, weighing up the dignity of its greatness in God's eyes, as you raise the harpoon for your small and often trivial human ends? And if you must raise it to sustain your life, do you pray that the nurturing of your life through the sacrifice of such a life as this will enrich the humility in your own human acclaim?

> Once we see, as is so obvious, that our knowledge is always partial and horrendously incomplete, we begin to perceive how very arrogant and dangerous [our human] confidence really is. The notion that the universe really is weird and is forever beyond our ken suggests that the only reasonable attitude towards it is absolutely not one of lordliness, but one of reverence. This is an ethical insight; and it comes from science as powerfully as from religion. They should be at one on this.
>
> Colin Tudge

The extended family: a new paradigm for human kinship

In the second chapter of his *Social Contract,* Rousseau identified the root of human ethical behaviour with our sense of kinship: we behave ethically towards those we recognise as family. We are not constrained by the same considerations in our dealings with those beyond the pale of that family circle. Social biology theory seeks to explain all of this neatly in terms of selfish genes: our family comprises those with whom we share the most genes.

At the heart of all the great religious traditions is a widening outwards of the bounding circle that defines family and community, further out than the reach of established or verifiable kinship, the web of relationships that can be depicted on a family tree. In this way my neighbour, whom I must love as myself, becomes all of mankind.[76] We need hardly go further than this to realise the limited extent to which we can call our society a Christian society. Indeed, the true religious concept of brotherhood is the very thing that must be bridled before religion can be harnessed in the service of the state in ways that are all too familiar from the study of history in every part of the world. The welcome accorded the total stranger in earlier times was a reflection of some latent instinct that there is a kinship beyond the visible boundary of parish and kingdom: the stranger might, in unsuspected and perhaps supernatural ways, be my kin. This is the tradition of all the great religions, from which it seeps out into society and politics: into concepts of the rights of man (Paine), Rousseau, Marx, the UN Declaration of Human Rights.

As foundation for the advance of spiritual instinct, which is the realisation of the notion of kinship with all mankind, we can of course now look to the biological discovery that we are in fact all related genetically – all mankind is one family. For people of faith in any of the great traditions there is such human enrichment in the expansion of consciousness and concern this brings about, that they scarcely feel the need to look further or deeper in an attempt to more fully understand who we are, or what God may be showing us about the ultimate meaning of things. In this way the stark, unadorned belief of faith can degenerate to credulity, hope becomes complacency and charity measurable.

This arrested exploration of who and what we are in the eyes of God can easily blind us to the relevance and significance of the incontrovertible demonstration by modern science of the extent to which all life is one family. In other words, other species are part of our 'we', and so the ripples of consanguinity must extend to all creatures, and with those expanding ripples the ethical imperative that is grounded in relationship. Theology has hardly begun to take account of the implications.

People identify more easily with the creatures that have most in common with us. In trying to decide their worth, we look for reflections of ourselves in them. And the more like us we think they behave, the more likely we are to consider whether they might have rights. We make ourselves the measure of their worth. We can see this in the way people often treat their pets. The more closely their response appears to approach the human, the more highly we value it. The activities of the ISPCA do not generally extend beyond warm-blooded vertebrates, though recent research is beginning to allow us a glimpse at a complexity of mind and behaviour in fishes hitherto unsuspected, by science at least, that may allow these more ancient vertebrates access to the family of creatures we warm to as kin.[77]

For those whom faith has gifted with the vision of meant harmony in all things, it is in their very existence that the primary value of other creatures lies, achieved in each species through a process of evolution exactly parallel to our own, each as unique as our own. Each is shaped by evolution for a unique mode of existence whose external parameters can be defined by ecology in terms of its niche. But there is a fire of awareness within for which our language can shape no words except in metaphor. With my human mind I can only penetrate so far in any attempt to reach their joy and sorrow, so different from mine: not in degree even, but in the very concept. The words for that joy are of necessity as far beyond our human conception as is the Unspoken Logos beyond our concepts of God in a different direction. The subjectivity through which insect and plant articulate their acclaim, as real as ours though it is, is effectively ineffable.

> *Ribes sanguineum*, the flowering currant,
> her back to the limestone wall and
> silent all winter, bursts
> into song in March, all bells and cymbals,

wind chimes and tinkle triangles,
calling the early bees to feast.

I expect you think
I have mixed my metaphors again:
as if carefully sorted figures of speech
and balanced syntax could get it right,
could frame the melody the flowering currant sang
with the morning light and the March wind
and the harkening Andrena
hastening.

And now I know
the answer to what we asked
each other often is where the currant sings
and swings its bells in the morning light,
never to be contained and held
in word. It does not need our words, it will
vanish with our attempts to name
its song.
                    Which is why
poetry succeeds, looking sideways
at the singing heart of the world.[78]

The awareness that is the dipper's acclaim is the adoration of a sister vertebrate of gentle ways, and we can bridge the distance between us in reaching for some understanding. But we are bewildered by nature red in tooth and claw (and redder still in sting and mandible) because we insist on applying to other beings the ethical standard by which our own behaviour must be judged. That standard comes with the gift that most sets us apart – reflective self-awareness and the capacity to understand. But with this capacity – because from those to whom most has been given most will be expected – comes the duty to exercise and develop this gift so that we become truly what we are meant to be. A part of that flowering is the development of compassion for all creatures, a virtue in the exercise of which perhaps we feel a faint, faint echo of the Great Need that calls creation into being in the first place. This is the First Commandment, given in what we are: 'Thou shalt love the Lord thy God with all thy heart, and with all thy soul, and with all thy mind, and with all thy strength': which means in its very essence loving the creation which is the only way we can come to know the Uncreated.

Here the indulgent unbeliever who has held onto the thread of the argument will let go, because the existence of Divine Goodness does not follow according to the threadbare logic of human argument. The wonderful complexity and ingenuity of life's diversity does not prove the existence of Ultimate Purpose. If it did we would be deprived of the critique of the great Richard Dawkins – to name but the favourite scapegoat of the theologian – and our debate would be the poorer.

Harmony in creation: towards a deeper ecology

Ecology is the science of the architecture of creation.

Albert Schweitzer

Ecology is a relatively new word, coined in 1866 by the German biologist Ernst Haeckel. It comes from the Greek word for house or home (*oikos*) – as do 'economy' and 'ecumenism.' Its main focus is the study of living things in their homes on earth, but we can extend our discussion to the edge of the science to consider the broader sense of being at home in the universe.

Species do not exist in isolation. The environment in which they live and for which their evolutionary history has honed their very precise relationship, is in a literal sense an extension of their lives and *vice versa* (see page 67). They draw their nourishment from it, and everything about them is determined by its opportunities and constraints. This network of environmental influences includes geology and soil, climate and topography, and it also includes the concatenation of other species, from microbes to predators, with which the life of the individual species is entwined. We catch a glimpse of a few of the threads in this concatenation when we study the trophic relationships modelled for us in 'food webs,' but these sets of relationships are immeasurably more complex than this.

Ecology today concentrates on the quantification and further elucidation of the details of these relationships and the processes involved, and is in this respect a scientific discipline governed by strict application of the criteria that govern the conduct and progress of all science. But of all the sciences, it is the one that conducts its business in closest proximity to creation as it comes to us direct from the Hand of God, and its practitioners are most subject to the pull of that emotional and spiritual gravity. The ecological curia polices any such tendencies diligently, and words such as harmony and holism are expurgated from its vocabulary: but in fact everything ecologists study and publish (wondering in unspoken amazement between the written lines) is the material surface expression of this deeper harmony.

The tradition of natural history out of which the modern science of ecology developed (a puritanical daughter committed to the spare virtue of its ascetic discipline) was utterly suffused with this sense of all-encompassing, inexpressibly wonder-inducing, harmony: and has left a rich legacy in the art and literature of the cultures in which it flourished. It is an accurate reflection of how we have distanced ourselves from encounter with creation that the volumes in which this rich tradition is preserved constitute a sort of modern Index of Forbidden (or at least forgotten) Books, gathering dust on the shelves of unvisited libraries.

The most ambitious attempt to establish the harmony and beauty to which naturalists, painters and poets responded on a more intellectual foundation was undertaken in the mid-nineteenth century by Alexander von Humboldt (1769-1859).[79] Von Humboldt was the greatest explorer and natural scientist of his day, extraordinarily widely travelled, a great adventurer, immensely intelligent and influential. His greatest work was *Cosmos*, which attempted nothing less than to bring together everything that was scientifically understood about the workings of the universe, but whose overarching aim was to demonstrate the scarcely fathomable harmony which von Humboldt believed, knew, sounded ever more symphonically the deeper our understanding of the world, the universe, about us grew. The capacity to respond to that harmony was something that was, is, instinct in us, something we all have naturally, and it is the task of science to augment and enhance that native sense of awareness of deeper harmony.

Part of the reason we hear little of von Humboldt nowadays is because Darwin's theory of evolution seemed to provide an adequate explanation for all this harmony in the world (*The*

Origin of Species was published the same year von Humboldt died). But in fact it was a reductionist explanation: the latest tragic dark flowering of the reductionism whose origin is usually attributed to Descartes back in the seventeenth century (the man who is blamed for reducing spirit to mechanism in western philosophy). You could nearly say the soul was taken out of the world.

Being dazzled by life's diversity

Thinking or reading about life's immense variety is one thing, but the experience of it is something else entirely. You can read about biodiversity in all the glorious books that are available to us today, or on the countless websites and TV programmes that we can access at the touch of a button. But that is mediated experience. We can only experience something of the reality of it through direct experience. When you look at the Tree of Life you see almost innumerable buds at the tips of twigs that proliferate from ever stouter branches as you approach the common trunk from which they all sprang in the dawn of life on earth. The buds are different groups of living things: reptiles or spiders or mosses, flowering plants or primates: each with a different biological blueprint, a different way of living, and so broadly similar from a distance. The spiders, for instance, all have smallish, hairy bodies divided into an abdomen at the rear with miraculous silk-spinning glands, a head-cum-thorax with six or eight eyes facing front and with distinctive fangs, and always eight legs.

But now, if we move up closer to the tree, we see that each bud is also a cluster of branchlets of greater or lesser density. And it is at this level of resolution, when we can see and compare individual species, that the diversity of life is at its most dazzling and we can gaze in awe and wonder at the unimaginable variety into which the more numerous groups have radiated. This, as Linnaeus' marvellous metaphor explains, is easier for us to appreciate in groups we can see easily with our eyes: the birds, for example, with more than 10,000 species that between them exploit every available corner of the earth available to birds, with every conceivable variation on the themes of wing and feather, beak and claw and all the unique things birds are inside, with colour and song to match. Or mammals, with their

4,500 species. But many groups of smaller animals have much greater numbers of species with body plans less familiar to the naked eye, and here the variety is mesmerising. 38,000 species of spiders (a class, just as birds are) have been described, and this is likely to be no more than a fraction of the total.

It is the same for flowering plants. No words can begin to convey the utterly dazzling variety of their most numerous families: especially perhaps the orchids (Orchidaceae), asclepiads (Asclepiadaceae) and the Asteraceae, the family to which daisies and dandelions belong. There are maybe 25,000 species of orchids, five times as many as mammals, and at least as many composites (the daisy-dandelion family). There are maybe 3,000 asclepiad species, but their complexity, diversity of shape and form, and beauty match the orchids. And the most amazing aspect of all this is that the variety and beauty appreciated by us are accidental: in the sense that each and every one has evolved to occupy a particular mode of living unique to itself: every detail of its design is functional and, as far as ecology goes, for itself.

The realisation of possibility
Each and every species is the realisation, i.e. the becoming real, of a possibility inherent in the very stuff of creation. But its very being depends upon its evolved capacity to function successfully in the particular environment it has chosen – or which chooses it. And it is this fact that makes the scale of living diversity so awesome. I remember some years ago having a conversation with a deeply religious friend of mine about biodiversity. We were discussing particularly wonderful instances of life's wonders when he remarked that if you can imagine it, God has already thought of it. But the wonder is on another plane entirely. The creatures on the drawing board of the imagination do not have to breathe and live in a real world. If we were to apply the criterion of real living to our imagined creatures, few of our candidate animals would translate into real beings. Yet the diversity of actual, real life surpasses anything our imagination could ever have devised. There is hardly a corner of the earth, however extreme or however small, to which different forms of life have not adapted themselves, often with almost unbelievable inventive-

The Insect Orders

Taxonomic Name	Common Name	Number Worldwide	Number in UK
The Apterygota (Wingless insects with no true metamorphosis at all)			
Thysanura	3-pronged Bristletails	55	9
Diplura	2-pronged Bristletails	600	11
Protura	Proturans	10	17
Collembola	Springtails	3000	300
The Exopterygota (Hemimetabolous insects with incomplete metamorphosis			
Ephemeroptera	Mayflies	2000	36
Odonata	Dragonflies and damselflies	5000	43
Plecoptera	Stoneflies	1700	34
Grylloblatodea		16	0
Orthoptera	Grasshoppers	20000	33
Phasmida	Stick insects	3000	3
Dermaptera	Earwigs	1200	5
Embioptera	Web spinners	300	0
Dictyoptera	Cockroaches and mantids	6000	4
Isoptera	Termites	1900	0
Zoraptera		22	0
Psocoptera	Book and bark lice	2000	68
Mallophaga	Biting lice	2800	225
Siphunculata	Sucking lice	300	61
Hemiptera	True bugs	100000	1410
Thysanoptera	Thrips	500	180
The Endopterygota (Holometabolous insects with complete metamorphosis)			
Neuroptera	Lacewings etc.	4 700	60
Mecoptera	Scorpion-flies	400	4
Siphonaptera	Fleas	1400	53
Coleoptera	Beetles	370000	3700
Strepsiptera	Stylops	370	16
Diptera	True Flies	100000	5700
Lepidoptera	Butterflies and moths	150000	2400
Trichoptera	Caddis-flies	5000	188
Hymenoptera	Ants, bees and wasps	120 000 +	

ness. Each species is a chord in the symphony of *achieved* being, not simply imagined being.

The form of encounter that is our experience of the living world demands of us a response that nurtures the realisation of further possibility. And there are two aspects to this response: care for that which has become real already, and development of the capacity for further possibility in each human, and that will take us into the realm of virtue (see page 162).[80]

Wonder before creation
Creation is intended for us in this sense: that our human capacity to understand is matched to its miraculous inherent intelligibility so that wonder kindles in us, as it will on whatever level of reality we focus our mind: the mathematics and physics of stars and atoms, the architecture and dance of chemical organisation, but surely nowhere more than in the unfolding of life's variety and complexity before our enquiring mind. The springtime, when this blossom of wonder should unfurl with greatest potential to later bear fruit and pass its treasure on to others, is in childhood. And this is why it is so essential that children have the experience of nature, and the guidance of 'at least one adult who can share it, rediscovering with him the joy, excitement and mystery of the world we live in.'[81] I will leave the words to the great, brave Rachel Carson (her last words to us).

> A child's world is fresh and new and beautiful, full of wonder and excitement. It is our misfortune that for most of us that clear-eyed vision, that true instinct for what is beautiful and awe-inspiring, is dimmed and even lost before we reach adulthood. If I had influence with the good fairy who is supposed to preside over the christening of all children I should ask that her gift to each child in the world be a sense of wonder so indestructible that it would last throughout life, as an unfailing antidote against the boredom and disenchantments of later years, the sterile preoccupation with things that are artificial, the alienation from the sources of our strength.
> What is the value of preserving and strengthening this sense of awe and wonder, this recognition of something

beyond the boundaries of human existence? Is the exploration of the natural world just a pleasant way to pass the golden hours of childhood or is there something deeper?

I am sure there is something much deeper, something lasting and significant. Those who dwell, as scientists or laymen, among the beauties and mysteries of the earth are never alone or weary of life. Whatever the vexations or concerns of their personal lives, their thoughts can find paths that lead to inner contentment and to renewed excitement in living. Those who contemplate the beauty of the earth find reserves of strength that will endure as long as life lasts. There is symbolic as well as actual beauty in the migration of the birds, the ebb and flow of the tides, the folded bud ready for the spring. There is something infinitely healing in the repeated refrains of nature – the assurance that dawn comes after night and spring after winter.[82]

Gaia

Life on earth has profound effects on the inanimate world it inhabits so all-pervasively. Life has been found in the most inhospitable environments on earth – even deep in solid rock.[83] Soil is a product of life; the chemistry of air and water are profoundly altered by life's activities. In 1979 James Lovelock put forward the hypothesis that life on earth acts, in what at times seems to be a purposeful way, to regulate the atmospheric envelope around it in order to sustain it in the condition best suited for its own continued maintenance – as though Life itself behaves like a great all-encompassing albeit unconscious organism.[84] The discoveries of the new science of ecophysiology over the last half century have put the concept beyond reasonable doubt, but there is much disagreement about how the living earth – personalised as Gaia in this new way of thinking, after the earth goddess of Greek mythology – is to be thought of. There is a spectrum of viewpoints that can be broken down into four overlapping interpretative bands: (1) life is so all-pervasive, interaction between it and the surrounding environment is inevitable and important; (2) life modifies the global environment; (3) life actually regulates the global environment; (4) life not only regulates the global environment, but does so purposefully, and with intent.[85] Whichever point of view we take, this new way of viewing the earth reinforces the need to think holistically in the management practices we adopt in our custodianship of the earth.

At the more 'religious' end of this spectrum Gaia is thought of as a goddess: the earth goddess of antiquity reincarnated in the language of science and armed with all the powers conferred on her by ecophysiology. In his earlier writing James Lovelock himself clearly thought of Gaia as something more than impersonal forces, but such was the opposition this aroused in more orthodox scientific circles he was tempted to distance himself from this way of thinking. The pressure from the opposite quarter was however more persuasive. In an article in *New Scientist* the renowned environmental writer Fred Pearse pleaded with Lovelock:

> Gaia as metaphor; Gaia as a catalyst for scientific enquiry; Gaia as literal truth; Gaia as earth Goddess. Whoever she is, let's keep her. If science cannot find room for the grand vision, if Gaia dare not speak her name in Nature, then shame on science. To recant now would be a terrible thing, Jim. Don't do it.[86]

While Lovelock constantly warns us not to think of Gaia as an organism in the way we usually do ('I am well aware that the term [life] itself is metaphorical and that the earth is not alive in the same way as you or me or even a bacterium'),[87] he still retains his belief that 'Gaia is a religious as well as a scientific concept, and in both spheres it is manageable … God and Gaia, theology and science, even physics and biology are not separate but a single way of thought.'[88] It is nonetheless important to retain the note of caution, so that our homage to what is one of the most important concepts of our age does not descend into a sort of ecological idolatry.

The progressive emergence of complexity[89]

> As we look out into the universe and identify the many accidents of physics and astronomy that have worked together to our benefit, it almost seems as if the universe must in some sense have known that we were coming.
>
> Freeman Dyson, *Disturbing the Universe*

The potential for complexity to develop or unfold on successively higher levels of organisation is *inherent* in the basic structure of matter. It is part of the *essence* of things.[90] Matter was created in the Big Bang, and at first it consisted almost entirely of hydrogen. But under certain conditions of temperature and pressure simple atoms of hydrogen combine to form the progressively more complex atoms of heavier elements. Until very recently we used to think the basic, irreducible building blocks of matter were protons, neutrons and electrons, but in recent decades science has been able to probe deeper, and we now know that these are made up of still smaller entities. At the leading edge of physics today scientists are straining to understand what the ultimate 'building blocks' of matter are, but we cannot form *meaningful* images of our mind at this level: our imagination is simply *not up to it*.

On certain planets, where the physico-chemical conditions are suitable, atoms of the same or different elements combine to form molecules, in accordance with chemical laws of which we have a good understanding. But the entirely new properties and behaviours that appear and diversify with the creation of atoms are not at all apparent at the organisational level of subatomic physics. The defining properties of the different chemical elements or compounds could not have been predicted from an understanding of their constituents. And those constituents are interchangeable: it is in the way different numbers of them are *arranged* and related that these new emergent properties are expressed.

Under the very special conditions found on the planet earth, the element carbon can exploit its unique capacity to bond so as to develop the ever more complex organic compounds that are the building blocks of living cells. The cell is almost unimaginably complex: but the defining life properties it exhibits are not something that could have been predicted from an understanding of the chemical components of which it is made, however comprehensive that understanding. The tendency to combine with other cells seems to be something that is inherent in cellular structure under certain conditions. This is accompanied by a progressive differentiation whereby different cells take on specialised functions: and so we are launched on the mesmerising journey of organic evolution through geological time. Eric J. Chaisson sees a form of natural selection for complexity at work not merely in organic evolution, but in the entire course of cosmic development.[91] This is a thought-provoking exposé of the way in which an inevitable direction is built into the fabric of the universe in a more strictly scientific way than the spirit-drenched and scientifically much less rigorous thinking of Teilhard de Chardin.

Natural selection does not in any sense explain the emergence of new properties of matter at successively higher levels of organisation. What compels belief in a 'designer' is the inherent potentiality of subatomic matter to evolve in such a way that at successively higher levels of association qualities that cannot be predicted from examination of the lower level of organisation emerge: and that on emergence, each successive property should explode into such awesome diversity and beauty: the diversity of form and properties of elements and compounds on the level of chemical organisation, biological diversity with the emergence of life and sentience, cultural efflorescence with the appearance of self-awareness. The more deeply we get to know these levels with the extensions of our senses modern science provides us with, the more compelling the argument becomes. What 'designer' might mean in this context is a further question, and essentially beyond any remotely adequate articulation.[92]

Atheistic critics such as Michael Shermer have attempted to engage with the challenge posed by the notion of emergent properties: but in a shallow and theoretical way. 'If life follows from [primordial] soup with causal dependability,' Paul Davies reflected in his wonderful book *The Fifth Miracle*, 'the laws of nature encode a hidden subtext, a cosmic imperative, which tells them: "Make life!" And, through life, its by-products: mind, knowledge, understanding. It means that the laws of the universe have engineered their own comprehension. This is a breathtaking vision of nature, magnificent and uplifting in its majestic sweep. I hope it is correct. It would be wonderful if it were correct.'[93] Michael Shermer's response to this is: 'Indeed, it would be wonderful. But not any more wonderful than if it were not correct … The cosmos may be one giant autocatalytic (self-driving) feedback loop that generates such emergent properties as life. We can think of self-organisation as an emergent property and emergence as a form of self-organisation. Complexity is so simple it can be put on a bumper sticker: LIFE HAPPENS.'[94]

What sort of response is this? As an exercise in logic such arguments might carry some weight – as an acceptable argument, say, as to why there should be something (anything) rather than nothing. But this is an argument that can only be made by someone who has not experienced or, more accurately, *encountered* reality. Such a response becomes possible when creation is not experienced for all that it is – for *all* that it is in the way that engenders that wonder which comes before explanation. This failure lay at the heart of the disagreement between Goethe and Newton over the nature of light – indeed, over the stature of science as we have come to practice it: as a discipline that establishes itself outside of the things it studies, detached from them, deliberately remote from the possibility of an encounter that is as subjective as it is objective.

While such detachment may be necessary in order to study the intelligible framework of things from quarks to minds, the intelligible face of reality is not its only aspect, and failure to return to the thing experienced once understanding is satisfied (for the moment, because the search for intelligibility is unending), is to have a comprehension of reality that is only partial, and that provides an incomplete grounding for any response as to its ultimate meaning: 'the best that the written word can be trusted for is to serve as a reminder of things that have already been experienced.'[95]

The ability to affirm a deeper meaning does not necessarily require a great deal of scientific understanding. The first impact of creation upon us is not generated by understanding but by its sheer ontological reality, which growing understanding deepens.

What it does require is a deeper mode of encounter with reality through which the meaning shifts into focus with an added dimension, as it were. The progress of science has, however, certainly expanded the horizons of seeing. The more science and technology enhance our capacity to see (albeit primarily with the aim of understanding) the more awesome the deeper encounter becomes also. In particular, the more closely we study the diversity of life, the more awe-inspiring the sheer extravagance of its diversity and beauty, intelligence and ingenuity encountered through this mode of seeing is. How marvellous it is that 'from so simple a beginning endless forms most beautiful and most wonderful have been and are being evolved' in orders of magnitude more marvellous than Darwin could ever have imagined.[96]

Science in the strict sense restricts itself to what can be measured, and lays great emphasis on the beauty of the mathematical expression that blossoms from such measurement. As James Jeans succinctly put it: 'From the intrinsic evidence of his creation, the Great Architect of the Universe now begins to appear as a pure mathematician.'[97] And yet this mathematical dimension is the most superficial (albeit the most deeply buried) aspect of the beauty of creation: other dimensions are simply less easy to quantify with the sophisticated rods and clocks of science.

To appreciate the overwhelming nature of the experience of life at this level of encounter we must pay attention to it, and for this attention all our senses are required. When we attend in this way we find that we have the capacity to truly appreciate only the tiniest corner of nature's kingdoms because of the sheer, endlessly amazing extravagance that only exposure to its detail in this way reveals. When reality is encountered in this mode, only an affirmation of its impact upon us that finds expression as worship is good enough. But precisely because it is essentially ineffable we find many different chords of affirmation in different cultures and at different times, across a spectrum of human response from Songlines to Nirvana, with Eucharist as some sort of central point. In attempting to articulate the encounter with reality, each elaborating theology freezes it lest it be lost – but reality cannot be transmitted in this frozen form: a theology can only point the Way.

A comparable argument could be made by those who study other levels of the organisation of matter: but it is especially significant at the level of biodiversity since it is this in which our sensory experience is enmeshed and embedded directly. It is on this level that the acceptance which is perhaps best represented initially by words such as 'acclaim' or 'assent' arises: that assent which bubbles up in the depths of our being and, when it reaches the surface struggles to express itself in words, but once we start using words we have started to define. This can be no more than the feeblest of metaphors: but just as the Heisenberg uncertainty principle means that the more accurately we define the position of an electron, the less accurately can we know its momentum, so it is with our affirmation of the ultimate Ground of Reality when we have to use words such as 'God'. Yet everything in human life hinges on this leap of assent that is 'faith in God'. Only when we have taken up a position on this are we ready to bring intellectual consideration to bear on such ethical or theological themes as 'virtue' or 'salvation': and the limits we have found in a purely intellectual approach to the question of 'God' should at least caution us against a purely intellectual interpretation of these themes.

The inadequacy of an encounter that divorces subject and object in the way of knowing of modern science is explored philosophically in the field of phenomenology, especially in the work of Husserl and Merleau Ponty, and more recently by such writers as Henri Bortoft and David Abram.[98] A further elaboration of phenomenology is required, however, to give adequate philosophical expression to some of these newer perspectives. Exposure to the tenets of phenomenology is not a pre-requisite for the capacity to affirm, however. All that we need is before all of us in everyday experience, although the possibility of its development and emergence is enhanced in surroundings dominated by natural rather than artificial phenomena.

There are much earlier intimations of the implicate enfolding of everything in the uninformed matter of the beginning of things. In the last sentence of his essay 'On a Piece of Chalk' – a sentence itself pregnant with implication – T. H. Huxley, Darwin's most articulate contemporary advocate and defender, wrote of how 'in the endless variation of the forms assumed by living beings, we have observed nothing but the natural product of the forces originally possessed by the substance of the universe.'[99] We also find an 'instinct' that creation consists of an evolutionary unfolding of initially undifferentiated potentiality through time in the thinking of some of the great theological minds of the early church. There are hints of it even as early as Irenaeus of Lyons (c. 130-200 AD), and later on in the writings of

Gregory of Tours (c. 538-594), but more especially in St Augustine, who seems to have envisaged – entirely without 'evidence' – that God in the beginning 'brought into existence a concentration of all energies and powers in which everything else was seminally contained. He then caused these energies to act according to their inherent laws. A reality pregnant with the future was created at the beginning of time, still formless, but already containing all forms of being within itself.'[100]

CHAPTER SIX

The Architecture of Creation: Mind

The emergence of mind

In the last chapter, great emphasis was placed on the unique achievement that is the individual species: the way in which each is the realisation – the making real of – an otherwise merely possible mode of existence. However, this is what a philosopher would call an ontological definition, which is not something the practising scientist can get his teeth into. To put the same thing in a more ecological way: each species occupies a unique environmental niche in time and space, which means that it has learned how to exploit a particular opportunity for living in a way no other has. No two species occupy the same niche indefinitely.[1] No matter how similar they appear, there is always some difference.

We can define these differences in environmental terms. As we have already seen, everything about a plant or animal is in a sense an extension of its environment and *vice versa*. But when we come to consider our human selves we find that, although this is just as true of us as it is of every other creature, we have something that is not just another adaptation that enables us to exploit the resources available to us more efficiently. We are not merely superbly aware in the way in which our animal cousins are, but we are aware that we are aware: *we know*. Our consciousness is reflective: *we can think*. In our species evolution has advanced another rung upwards on the ladder of material possibility: a new potential of matter has been realised at the level of neural organisation reached in certain groups of primates. And however amazing it is that the properties of life and feeling should have been inherent in the very structure of matter from the beginning, it is even more so that reflective consciousness should have been inherent in it. 'It is profoundly puzzling how [consciousness] could come about from the seemingly purely calculational, unfeeling and utterly impersonal laws of physics that appear to govern the behaviour of material things.'[2]

We are of course very conscious that we humans are unique. We are so aware of it that for a long time we thought of ourselves as altogether superior because of this special human talent, in the process losing sight of our place in creation, so firmly were our eyes fixed on a destiny that would see us enjoying eternity with God, in whose image we conceived ourselves to be made – unmindful of the fact that so is every other creature on earth. Now we know better. There is a greater humility in our attitude, but it is – or it can and should be – accompanied by a boundless exhilaration at our re-discovery of the long-forgotten family to which we belong, and we can now return to ask the question of what is special about the human mode of being in a more essential way: what is this special human talent, and how are we meant to use it, knowing our place in creation as we now do, and having a better grasp of family history?

We are no less a part of the family than before, but we have been promoted to a new post of responsibility in the family, so to speak. If our living, in common with all that lives but in a way distinct to us, can in some sense be thought of as sharing in an incomprehensible well-spring of life that out of infinity infuses the cosmos (we might call it the Divine Life), we can through this new human mode of apprehension be said in some sense to share in the Divine Mind.[3]

Creation is the absolute revelation, the very embodiment of divinity, 'the primary revelation of that ultimate mystery whence all things emerge into being':[4] not in the sense that a book might be, but *through it and in it* we experience God. For many people indeed, 'nature' is God, and many who would hesitate to use the word God are often conscious of being enfolded by nature in a deeper way than the biophilia hypothesis can explain. Nor is it necessary for us to use the word God as if it were a sort of key that lets us explore these depths. The God concept is so anthropomorphically burdened, we may come closer to the reality by shedding it: it is not through failure of intelligence or reflection that it is absent from much of the philosophy and vocabulary of the Far East (see page 126).

* * *

How should we respond then? The fountainhead of our response is the *awe* that awakened within us as the world came into focus in this new way with the birth of our kind. The dawning of reflective consciousness was like the clearing of a foggy mirror or window. We have embarked on a new stage of our journey: not just our journey, because all of life has come this far with us. What we have been given through this gift is an altogether new and richer way of knowing and relating to the world: the ability to be embraced by the *real presence* of the reality we call God in an altogether deeper way, as deeply as our limited capacities will allow. It is given to us to experience the presence of God in such a way that we can relate through intelligence to what he is about in creation – to touch ever so distantly the hem of his joy and beauty and personhood. This is what Pope Benedict means when he says that 'Between God and us … there exists a real analogy, in which … unlikeness remains infinitely greater than likeness, yet not to the point of abolishing analogy and its language.'[5]

This is the acclaim we are called to: spellbound by creation to add the echo of our enchanted response to the symphony of nature's chorus. But while the journey and the prospect are thrilling beyond measure, they carry a price, because with them comes the opportunity and the capacity to use our minds to bring profound change to the world, and we bear the responsibility of using that capacity to further the harmony of creation achieved through four billion years of life's becoming. What we are about in the world in our day is, in large measure, a turning away from this invitation: because what follows from all of this is that it is a sin to commit a crime against the natural world:

> For humans to cause species to become extinct and so destroy the biological diversity of God's creation … for humans to degrade the integrity of earth by causing changes in its climate, by stripping the earth of its natural forests, or destroying its wetlands … for humans to injure other humans with disease … for humans to contaminate the earth's waters, its land, its air, and its life, with poisonous substances … these are sins.[6]

There is therefore a moral dimension to our efforts to sustain the diversity, beauty and integrity of creation wherever it comes within reach of our influence. We need to live in a world where we can be enchanted by creation, as we are made to be.[7]

We pray and worship in our different ways, each with the voice the Lord has given us. The talent we are given to this end is different in kind from that given to other creatures. It enables us to look further and deeper than the limits of our ape's senses. It enables us to add the response of human intelligence to the acclaim of the universe. There may well be other rational intelligences elsewhere in the universe in this choir, including ones that go beyond us. We don't know, and perhaps we never will.

The dawn of consciousness

Consciousness endows us with the capacity to seek the story, the explanation. And in parallel with this is the question of how I am expected to respond in practice. What is right living in the light of this, in relation to myself, in relation to my community? Story and praxis evolve in time, blossoming into culture, some-times on to civilisation. But civilisation for all its achievement, is brittle, distanced from the well-spring, inflexible. It can only be for its time and place. As long as the well-spring is there, we can always return. There is an upward arrow of progress both in story and in praxis. We take the best of both with us as we move forward, ever-returning to refine. All story and culture up to now have been regional (bioregional), necessary perhaps to maintain the anchor in nature. Two of today's great problems are that regionalism has broken down, much of its achievement lost; and the cord to nature is fraying. Part of the great challenge of our time is how to save the achievement of national, regional and local culture, while at the same time weaving the New Story of creation for mankind as a whole.

CHAPTER SEVEN

A deeper mode of scientific encounter

As nothing is more easy than to think, so nothing is more difficult than to think well.

Thomas Traherne, *First Century*, Meditation 8

The questioning that may result in an understanding of the
mechanism whereby a particular part or aspect of reality *works* is
only one facet of the human encounter with creation. It is, however, the facet that tends to dominate in our culture. But the
understanding that results is as it were filtered from the primary,
immediate, sensory confrontation through which creation ex-
poses itself to us. A particular facet of creation (a particular plant
or animal, say) reveals or manifests itself to us through a unique
sensory spectrum, but is apprehended differently by other
modes of existence. Each species is equipped for a sensory response unique to itself and its specific mode of existence. We can
only apprehend a fraction of its total manifestation, the way it
communicates with other beings in its surroundings. Any one
species apprehends only that fraction of the total manifestation
that is relevant to its own existence: the 'filtering apparatus' of
each species is unique to itself (see below, page 120).

In the first place then, our capacity to register the full
panoply of sensory stimuli is restricted by the very limited
capacity of our human sensory apparatus. But over and beyond
this, our capacity to respond to the full message of the sensory to
the best of our limited ability is dampened, at times to the point
of being smothered, by the way our questioning mind has short-
circuited it, focusing its attention on what we sense with our
eyes (the sense most closely allied with mind). The full sensory
encounter is telling us more than intellect itself can abstract,
since this is only concerned with mechanism, the rational basis
of its workings, and that abstraction may not be sufficient when,
at the end of our enquiry into things, we come to ask one or

other variant of the question of what it all means, what it is all about. So we need to recover our openness to the full message of the sensory. This is not easy, because like muscles that we have not used for a long time if we are laid up in bed, the faculties we need are weak from lack of use.

Sensory experience results in *feelings*, which are psychological. They are, if you like, our overall response to what all the senses tell us, and they are the foundation upon which we base our values. At the same time though, our mind is reaching more deeply into the experience and touching something deeper, and finding echoes that awaken a response in us on a level that finds no words. This *intuition* reaches back for deeper meaning, by way of what Jung referred to as 'unconscious contents and connections.' We reach out in an attempt to perceive the thing as a new and unique and different presence to the world, independent of us in its being and worth, and then attempt to relate to what it is for itself, apprehending it as a presence within oneself, and not only as an object entirely outside one's own being.[1] Sensation and intuition are *perceptive*, independent of evaluation and understanding. They are, however, the foundation in which understanding and valuation are grounded.[2]

To the reductionist mind intuition is deeply suspect, although its role in the mental processes involved in scientific enquiry is widely recognised.[3] This intuition is not some kind of vague instinct but something with which our questing mind touches in a distinct way when we probe reality in this deeper encounter. The word comes from the Latin *intuere*, to cut into – it involves penetration to the very heart of the thing, but the instrument with which we probe is the mind entire, not our senses alone nor our disembodied intellect, and what we intuit is not readily subjected to measurement by the calipers of science that compute length and breadth, time and distance; nor indeed is what it touches some extra dimension, but the presence of that wavelength – for want of an adequate word – through which the Ground of Being is involved in being. It is as though I hear an echo of an almost infinitely distant sound – except that it is whatever corresponds to an echo in the vocabulary of mind.

What this fuller sensuousness touches generates a sensory confrontation and experience of altogether greater richness, from which thinking, writing and speaking have increasingly divorced us and made difficult of access. Yet it is primarily through such experience of the natural world that we apprehend a fuller dimensionality to reality, and it is this that has the capacity to transform our perception of its meaning.

This conversion may be sudden, striking us all at once from the horse of reductionist certainty, or it may be gradual, an endless progress into a deeper realm of experience whose starting point is the feeling of which Byron writes in *Childe Harold*, and is echoed over and over by all who have sensitively attempted to chronicle an experience that is, nonetheless, essentially ineffable.

> There is a pleasure in the pathless woods,
> There is a rapture on the lonely shore.
> There is society where none intrudes,
> By the deep Sea, and music in its roar:
> I love not Man the less but Nature more,
> From these our interviews in which to steal
> From all I may be, or have been before,
> To mingle with the Universe, and feel
> What I can ne'er express, yet cannot all conceal.[4]

We are trying here to recover a deeper, more ancestral, animistic perception for which our adoption of thinking, speaking and writing have substituted. That faculty has atrophied on this account, but it is a faculty we need for a more adequate confrontation with our countless brothers and sisters in all their diverse modes of being, which cannot communicate with us through the medium of human words. We need to recover this if we are ever really going to appreciate what is meant by the idea that creation is a communion of subjects rather than a collection of objects, or heal the split in ourselves between *res cogitans* and *res extensa* formalised by Descartes. This is about participating in the communion of the *anima mundi*: 'When we try to pick out anything by itself, we find it hitched to everything else in the universe.'[5]

For many scientists, the measurable behaviour of matter explains everything. There is nothing beyond the equations that explain the way the thing works, whether we are considering light, gravity, life or mind. The mode of explanation that confines itself to what the intelligence filters from sensory apprehension in this way is what we mean by *mechanism*. People who believe the mechanical explanation is the full explanation are often, as it were, 'colour-blind' to the values that rest upon a deeper mode of awareness. To take a significant example, Charles Darwin (who so thrilled, for instance, to the extraordinary ingenuity of the mechanical contrivances whereby orchids effect pollination, and who did more than anyone else to elucidate these contrivances) had no comparable appreciation of literature or art. Here is an extraordinary sentence from his autobiography: 'I have tried lately to read Shakespeare, and found it so intolerably dull that it nauseated me.' When he was asked after his visit to the Louvre in Paris what he had thought of it, Darwin replied – apparently not tongue in cheek – that he had seen some very fine frames.

All of this is very hard to explain in words because words are *exactly* what it is not about. But the fact that it is difficult to articulate properly doesn't mean it is a mere figment of the imagination. No, it is an intuitive recognition (*re-cognitio*) of shared relationship, shared history, shared being.

Thought tends to dampen down the fullness of this sensory experience, and the feelings to which it gives rise, and to freeze the delicate reach of intuition. Quantification in particular, which is essential to a scientific understanding of how a thing works, detaches us from the more holistic mode of enquiry – it is concerned only with matter, not form, in the Aristotelian and Thomist sense of these concepts. The development in the human species of self-reflective thought and language is really an abstraction from the primary holistic response and can be interpreted as a form of imprisonment or banishment. But even for those aspects that are amenable to explanation (by the intellect), our expression of that explanation in thoughts and words can only be part of the whole, because that which we explain in this way was not conceived/invented in thought and word (think of the pollination strategies of flowers, or spore dispersal in fungi).

It is in the light of that fuller experience of reality that we should ask: *What is going on?* The most immediately accessible part of the answer to that question concerns the way things work, and we need neither feelings nor intuition to answer this;

it is concerned with deducing observable laws that can be measured and expressed verbally or mathematically. But there is more to the experience than this – we have to extrapolate, to filter the intelligible out from that 'more' to formulate our mechanical explanation.

When you hear a robin sing, the sound penetrates instantaneously to feeling and intuition so that thought is for a moment by-passed. Or how you feel when you gaze at a flower, or spectacular scenery? These responses are irrelevant to the question of how flowers or landscapes work. But to forget or leave our initial response behind when we come to ask questions about how things work is to cut ourselves off from what is being said to us.

The answer we arrive at to the question of 'ultimate meaning' (the question is not framed in words and neither is the answer) is rather a disposition, an attitude for which we may (for want of a more adequate word maybe) call *acclaim*. It is not to be found at the end of the almost unimaginably sophisticated intellectual journeys science is embarked upon in its search for 'ultimate' answers, because these are still arrived at by means of the network of pathways that began with the question of how things work. We are called upon as humans to make this intellectual journey. It has brought us into strange territory (the search for a theory of everything that is). It may indeed be that we can describe this journey as an attempt to understand something of the 'Mind of God;' but it may be too that humility (in the sense in which that virtue was once understood, of knowing our place in the universe) is harder to find in that rarified air, and we are more likely to catch the infection of the Lucifer syndrome.

On the other hand, the added element of understanding filters back in a feedback loop *to reinforce intuition*, uniquely enriching the human response so that it is now more than a cry, it is *hosanna*. Intellect enriches intuition, feeling and acclaim, but intellect can search out its explanations only at the level of individual details, and only in order to answer the question of how things work. It must, as it were, detach itself from the other modes of enquiry in order to do this.

When we experience the creation (= the observable universe)

in this more open, deeper way, it is only natural for us to respond in a worshipful way.[6] All creatures respond in a worshipful way in this sense, each acclaiming their unique life with a different response; but in our human case there is something new – our understanding takes that response onto a new level that finds expression ritually in the endlessly varied ways that have evolved in different cultures, and intellectually in the spectrum of religious thought and discourse.

One of the feelings that are at the root of the religious 'response' is the sense of awe before creation. That can occur in many contexts – immediately and familiarly when we are confronted with tremendous scenery for instance (I well remember the sense of being gobsmacked by the awesome scale of the Alps after years spent coming to know the mountains of Slieve Bloom). It was the process of coming to terms with that kind of experience that gave birth to the Romantic movement. When we are confronted by vastness in this way our minds need to make an accommodation that enables us to be able to take it into the limited vessels our evolution has equipped us with. Our imaginations are able to penetrate the depth of creation's vastness only so far in every instance. Science brings vastness before us at both ends of the scales of time, distance, size and visibility. The cosmic end is one we get to think about a lot these days as more and more data pour in from the Hubble telescope. Ptolemaic spheres and epicycles were the intellectual devices through which the medievals accommodated their sense of the vastness. We know it to be so much more, but once you get beyond a certain level our senses can't distinguish 'degrees of vastness.' Our accommodation is the taxonomy of astronomy and stellar evolution. But at the far end of the possible experience of vastness is confrontation with the vastness of what is implied by the notion of 'God'. Our accommodations here are religion – and theology as a poor attempt of our intellect to come to terms with what religion is a response to.[8]

A fuller apprehension

Most of the time the things of creation merely touch the fringes of our attention. We do not attend to them in the way that is required in order to know what they are about in the world, neither on a sensory level or on an emotional level, or on an intellectual level. Take the moss on the trunk of a tree for instance. I scarcely see it; I hardly noticed it until my attention was drawn to it just now. I haven't a clue as to its name or who its relatives might be. I do not look closely enough to see the shape of its leaves, aglow with the special pale green with which they intercept the light of the sun, nor the beauty of its spore capsules, to say nothing of its internal structure and chemistry. I have no idea what slot it occupies in the jigsaw of its habitat. I know nothing of its history, the journey that has taken its ancestors through geological time on a journey as evocative as my own. Not attending to these things, I cannot respond to its meaning.

It would take a lifetime to appreciate this moss for what it is. On earth today there are somewhere between 10,000 and 15,000 different species of mosses. How many lifetimes would it take to even begin to know them all? And of course I can repeat this exercise for every group of living things – for earth stars and water bears, sea cucumbers and sharks, lichens and moths, for every kin group that has a room in Linnaeus' great mansion, and then start all over again for any geological period my informed imagination can transport me back to.

What does this alert attention, this deeper mode of encounter entail? The first problem you will encounter is the difficulty of simply finding time for it. We are constantly busy, even our leisure time is ruled by the clock. We flit from activity to activity, seldom absorbed in one thing for long before we are thinking about what we have to do next. But if you are to get to the heart of things, contemplation is called for.

When you seek to apprehend some new aspect of reality (this new flower for example), different faculties are involved. Understanding how it works, what its history is, its ecology, its chemistry, is only one of them. Hold that in abeyance for the moment, because the mental operations involved in coming to understand the how of it tend to smother the operation of the other faculties, shout them down, as it were, so you can't hear them. The first and most immediate aspect of your encounter with the flower is purely sensory. But you need to use your senses *as fully as you can* to apprehend the physical and chemical messages it is sending you. You need to take your time over this, let it soak into you. And you must do it alone, in silence.

Sight

Of the five senses that mediate our experience and understanding of the world, sight is much the most powerful, and it is the one most closely allied with our capacity to understand. This often means that not only are we not fully alert to the part of the messages coming to us through the other senses, but the questions that begin to form in our minds as soon as we look at something weaken the full impact of the visual image. The poet or artist in whose mind the business of understanding how it works is not uppermost will see further, be more responsive for example to the sensory experience of colour, form or positional relationships.

When we encounter an object such as this flower, our sight is usually the primary way in which we sense it, but our visual inspection is seldom more than casual. Use your sight now to apprehend its form in as much detail as you can see – the burnished colour of its petals, the form of the stamens. Augment what your naked eye can see with the enhanced vision a hand lens gives you.

For all our keenness of eye, many animals have much sharper eyes than ours. Eagles and hawks can see as much as eight times more clearly than we can: an eagle can spot a hare from a mile away. And apart from the enhanced acuity that enables certain animals to see so much more sharply than we do, there are animals that can see areas of the electromagnetic spectrum to which we are blind. Bees can see ultraviolet light; flowers that are one colour to us are something we can't even imagine to them. And rattlesnakes can 'see' the infrared that accompanies the body heat of their warm-blooded prey in the 'dark'.

Smell

Smell with your eyes closed at first. If in evolutionary terms sight is the most recently elaborated of our senses, smell is the most deeply rooted, the most ancient. As W. H. Hudson put it, 'The books tell us that sight, the most important of our senses, is the most intellectual; while smell, the least important, is in man the most emotional sense.' When you enter a wood you become more conscious of nature's scents than you normally do as you go about your everyday life in home, workplace or classroom.

The smell of the wood is an immensely complex mixture of things, because most of the communicating in the wood is being done chemically. Many are by-products of the busy activity of fungi and bacteria in the soil but most appear to be produced by the trees themselves, for reasons nobody is really sure about, and although the messages are seldom intended for our noses in any primary way, we respond to them. At any season the air in woods is different, special, whether it is still or whispering through the leaves or swirling through the winter branches. It is only ten to fifteen years ago that researchers first started to seriously analyse the air of the forest and discovered (in one instance) that it contained 120 chemical compounds of which 50 were hitherto unknown substances. The Japanese, who appreciate their trees more than most peoples, have a special word for the feeling of walking through the air of the forest: *shinrin-yoku*, wood-air bathing.[9]

If the streams of scent in the wood could be translated into false colour, the way electromagnetic signals above or below the visible spectrum often are to let us see what is actually there but invisible to us, the air in the wood would be a veritable multidimensional kaleidoscope, its patterns swirling and eddying about us mesmerically.

Our ability to pick up on these chemical messages is very weak in comparison to other creatures whose sense of smell is more attuned to them in the way our eyes are attuned to the narrow visible part of the electromagnetic spectrum. Most mammals are less attuned visually then we are, but more sensitive than us in other ways. Dogs have a level of smell that is said to be a thousand times greater than that of humans; where we have 5 million olfactory receptors in our nose, a dog has more than 220 million. But even this is as nothing compared with some insects. The tiny predatory wasp *Microplitis croceipes* uses smell to locate the caterpillars of the corn earworm on which it lays its eggs. It can pick up the smell of its prey at concentrations of one in a thousand billion – 100,000 times weaker than the lowest concentrations detectable by artificial, commercial 'electronic noses'.[10]

Sound
It is much the same with hearing. Our ability here also lies some-

where in the middle of the wide spectrum of sensitivity to the vibrations of the atmosphere and other sound wave-conducting media that constitutes hearing. And just as there are animals that can see colours to which we are blind, so too there are animals that hear frequencies to which we are deaf. Not only can dogs hear sounds four times better than we can, but they hear across a range of frequencies that is twice as wide as ours. Bats apprehend ultrasound signals that are inaudible to us – in effect they 'see' with their ears in the sense that they use ultrasound to form a 'sound-picture' that is as clear an impression of the object to them as the light-picture our eyes provide us with – an idea that was scoffed at for a century and a half after it was first suggested in 1794 by Lazaro Spalanzani.[11] The ears of invertebrate animals further away from us on the evolutionary scale may be entirely different to ours. Insects and spiders for example 'hear' by means of a complex array of spines, hairs and pits on their legs and elsewhere.

However, there is more to hearing than the measurable ability to sense sound waves. A particular sound may be a key that unlocks memory, and brings to life in the present past experiences that were hidden away until that sound released them. What is released may at times have its roots deeper than conscious memory and, it may be, deeper than the memory that originates in individual experience (see page 114).

As often as not, it is not our limited aural acuity that makes us deaf to something, but the fact that we are not listening. It is unlikely you can tell me what birds you heard singing the last time you went for a walk. And in our day we are so constantly assaulted with noise that we need this ability to cut out unwanted sound to maintain our sanity. There is so much noise it is difficult to hear the smaller natural sounds that carry so much meaning for us, and which convey intimations of deeper meaning.[12] When God visited Elijah in the wilderness his voice was not in the sound of thunder:

> And, behold, the Lord passed by, and a great and strong wind rent the mountains, and brake in pieces the rocks before the Lord; but the Lord was not in the wind: and after the wind an earthquake; but the Lord was not in the earthquake: And after the earthquake a fire; but the Lord was not in the fire: and after the fire a still small voice.

And it was so, when Elijah heard it, that he wrapped his face in his mantle, and went out, and stood in the entering in of the cave. And, behold, there came a voice unto him, and said, 'What doest thou here, Elijah?'[13]

It is not so much, at times, that we cannot hear ourselves think. It is that we cannot hear because of our thinking. It is only when we can hold our thoughts in abeyance that we can fully apprehend the meaning being conveyed to us by the sounds of creation. The song of Thoreau's robin penetrates instantaneously to feeling and intuition so that thought is for a moment by-passed.

That instinctive state of the human mind, when the higher faculties appear to be non-existent, a state of intense alertness and preparedness, which compels the man to watch and listen and go silently and stealthily, must be like that of the lower animals: the brain is then like a highly-polished mirror, in which all visible nature – every hill, tree, leaf – is reflected with miraculous clearness; and we can imagine that if the animal could think and reason, thought would be superfluous and a hindrance, since it would dim that bright perception on which his safety depends.[14]

Touch and taste
Touch and taste are the least versatile instruments – the tympani perhaps – of the orchestra of human sensation, but they seldom have to perform alone. In combination with the other instruments they are capable of lending an extraordinary new versatility to the symphony, and on their own, at times, may be as vocal and meaning-filled as the silence out of which God spoke to Elijah in the wilderness.

All life is the present moment
Your experience of the flower is the experience of this moment, in which time is merely another dimension of its being. There is only now. 'Time itself, the fourth dimension, does not "pass" but is laid out forever like a landscape: another ancient notion that has now achieved scientific respectability.'[15] Look at this tree. It gathers all of the past into itself so that time becomes space in this present moment: its form, and the rings in its trunk

and branches articulate the years of its individual life, as its specific essence does the eons of its geological journey. It draws all of the future towards itself in anticipation – its fruiting drawing next year and the next generation in, its evolution open-ended possibility yet conditioned by the achievement it brings into the present. But only the present moment into which these flow is alive and to be experienced.[16]

CHAPTER EIGHT

The ground of being

Affirming God

> Hence the existence of God, in so far as it is not self-evident to us, can be demonstrated from those of his effects which are known to us.
>
> Thomas Aquinas, *Summa Theologiae*, Part 1, Section 2, Article 2

> In this life we cannot see God's substance but know him only from creatures ... So this is where our words for God come from: from creatures.
>
> Thomas Aquinas, *Summa Theologiae*, Part 1a, Section 13

If our experience and intuition of the world leads us to the conviction that we live in a created universe, that our universe is *meant*, that there is some ultimate purpose at work, what more can we say? In words, apparently, not much that is reliable, because as soon as we do the wordless acclaim that rises as response from the depths of our being fragments into a multitude of different concepts, all radically restricted by what we are by virtue of our biological nature, and by cultural conditioning. Restricted by what we are first of all, because we can only feel and imagine using the sensory equipment with which evolution has endowed us to lead the life of an intelligent ape. Any notion we might have of what God is must simply be unspeakably inadequate.

We need at this point to clarify the notion behind that most problematic of words, 'God'. If the word 'atom' is a problem for our understanding, how will we fare with words at this other end of the scale of being and meaning?[1] Our European image of God is profoundly influenced by our first glimpse of him in Genesis. That image becomes imprinted on our minds, and ever after we are like Lorenz' geese![2]

Asking what kind of God is 'behind' it all is to call for an image, and there can be no image, neither in pictures nor in words. As we have already seen, our biological capacities have been sharpened by evolution to fit us for a particular niche on the earth (see page 67). What we intend by the concept of God, by the word itself, is utterly beyond anything we can conceive or speak of. When we feel compelled to talk about God our words are the babbling of a child. And although every attempt is immediately inadequate, we have this compulsion to do the best we can. To say anything is immediately to limit and there is no limit to God. Even to say that is to further limit him, because the very word 'limit' is intended to apply to creatures, things and processes such as we ourselves are. Needless to say, to speak of God as *him* is profoundly limiting, but *her* or *them* are no better, so we might as well stick to one or the other.

Even the great Thomas Aquinas, who wrote at such length of God's attributes, is at pains to point out that when we speak of God's goodness, or power or whatever, we are speaking analogously, in metaphors, every positive statement limited by our very speech. The only positive statements we can make with confidence are negative ones: 'The most we can say about God is that we do not know him.' Indeed, we cannot rightly speak of God's existence because everything that 'exists' (insofar as we can understand the word) is finite. We can therefore truly say that God does not exist.[3] 'This battle of words,' St Augustine wrote at one point, 'should be avoided by keeping silent.'[4] This *via negativa* or negative way of speaking of God – what is referred to as 'apophatic theology' – is profoundly embedded in all the main religious traditions, though emphasised in some much more than in others.

Would it be better to jettison the word God, laden as it is with the outworn baggage of millennia of trying to understand what it is all about, if only to facilitate our Christian dialogue with the religious traditions of the East? Indeed, it is not just atheists who want to abandon the word, so do some theologians.[5] But what better word will we find? Martin Buber argued passionately for the retention of this 'most loaded of all human words', upon which 'the generations of human beings have foisted the burden of their tormented lives … and pressed it into the ground' … 'We cannot wash the word "God" clean, and we cannot make it whole; but we can raise it from the ground, stained and torn to pieces as it is, and set it up over an hour of great anxiety.'[6]

Silence is the alternative. And indeed, in the end, we may find, as so many have found, that it is the better alternative. When Van Gogh felt what he described as 'a terrible need … shall I say the word? … of religion,' his response was to 'go out at night and paint the stars'.

There are good reasons for atheism if the God in question is the God of people such as Richard Dawkins, Daniel Dennett and Christopher Hitchins. Anyone who professes faith in God today must be as forthright as they are in their condemnation of all the evil that has been perpetrated in the name of religion over the centuries, and continues in our own day. We cannot be any less distrustful than Hitchens of 'anything that contradicts science or outrages reason.'[7] But this God of whom we speak is not the God people like Hitchens condemn in their attacks on religion. What they rightly condemn is an idol, a false god, or a pantheon of false gods. The true God was somewhere at the heart of it once, but has been smothered by human failure to follow heart and head. And yet he is not absent, but so deeply present, so intimately involved that we do not see him; but as it were constantly intimate his presence in the design of the world, in the mathematical, chemical, biological, aesthetic and spiritual architecture and beauty of the patterns that progressively unfold through emergent probability.

Words or concepts – the necessary tools of discourse – are shaped by culture and upbringing. In this search for words to express what we mean, we are no longer on the sure ground of science in the stricter and narrower sense of mechanical explanation. Once we embark on the building of this tower of words and concepts, 'whose top may reach unto heaven' so that 'nothing may be restrained from [us], which [we] have imagined to do,'[8] different communities of discourse will inevitably weave different stories of their words.

But we must construct our towers of words as best we may, in the languages we are born with, in the culture and religion we are born to, and grow out of them, as infants grow. Our capacity to construct such towers grows slowly over time. In the land of Sminar of old they could only construct their Tower of Babel using 'brick for stone, and slime for mortar'. Our towers are computers. Who can tell what towers our children may build in their attempt to reach unto heaven a century hence, a thousand years from now? 'Provided we have no cosmic or man-made disaster, we should, on this earth alone, still have more than a thousand million years of evolution in front of us.'[9]

Denying God

Je n'ai pas besoin de cette hypothèse.
                                        Laplace

But of course, here's the rub. Although some of the greatest minds have applied themselves to arguing the existence of God (and they don't come much greater than Augustine, Aquinas and Lonergan), other great minds disagree. How can it be that so many brilliant people fail to recognise an intelligence at work, fail to see any Great Work of intention, any Grand Design woven with a filigree of the good and beautiful. We struggle hopelessly in our search for words to encapsulate the concept; our greatest minds cannot agree whether it is personal or impersonal. How is it that so many of the brightest minds of our age and every age fail to see something so fundamental, which the peasant in the fields can see? Is the latter deluded, is it a hangover from the childhood of the human species that we must find the strength to grow out of without losing the moral fibre to hold society to-gether? How can somebody as good and intelligent as (to name some favourite examples) Richard Dawkins, Michael Sherman or Julian Huxley not see?

Those coloured holograms that were especially popular a few years ago may provide a helpful metaphor. You are presented with a brilliantly coloured drawing of swirling patterns and patches, but there is no pattern. But if you stare at it for long enough in a certain way it suddenly snaps into focus, and you see in all its shockingly sharp three-dimensionality a tiger, a pre-cipitous mountain or whatever meaning was hidden from you. It was there all the time but you couldn't see it. Some people never see it. It has nothing to do with intelligence, but more like a capacity on a deeper level to appreciate the holism hiding within.

The argument is made, powerfully, passionately and with great intellectual conviction by many influential and important scientists, that everything is explained by the mechanisms of evolution.[10] Reason operating alone through the *modus operandi* of science as we have come to practice it with such enormous success has, we are told, made God redundant. Darwin, at the time of his famous voyage on the Beagle a devout believer, gradually became an atheist in later life. Others, however, journey in the opposite direction. Anthony Flew was one of the most influential atheistic philosophers of the second half of the 20th century. In recent years he has revised his perspective, his *weltannschaung*, and believes the most rational explanation for the universe is that it was created by God.[11] So how are we lesser mortals to know what end of the 'magnet of response' is the correct one? If the most sincere and intelligent people can arrive at such different perspectives on Ultimate Reality, how can we be certain of anything in this area?

Atheism is only possible where individual human encounter with reality is limited, less than it should be, and tied to a mode of scientific enquiry that is blind to the implications of the fact that we cannot predict in advance what properties will emerge at progressively higher levels of material organisation, because these properties do not manifest themselves in advance. There are many causes for this blindness: upbringing or choice, chance or necessity, physiology or temperament.

And because this is the cause, it is very difficult to convert its proponents, especially as many of these are 'first rate minds', many of them wonderful writers, some of them verbal Houdinis – and so much of what they write is constructive and true. And yet, somebody who is not in the same league intellectually can 'see the picture' in the hologram of reality at a glance, because of a greater openness to the richness of experience, but feel daunted when 'superior' minds pour scorn on his simplicity. At the same time, however, many others who would not claim to be first rate minds have abandoned the religion in which they grew up, and are content to follow the lead of these articulate atheistic men of science.

I have attempted in a previous section to elucidate the shallow depth to which the scientific enquiry into the nature of reality penetrates, for all its sophistication. And there is now an extensive literature of response from theologians, philosophers and scientists to the virulent anti-religious atheistic stance of

Dawkins, Dennett, Hitchins and others – people find the stance of Dawkins inadequate.[12] Of its very nature the atheistic stance of Dawkins and others obviates the need to look for anything deeper than a mechanistic explanation of how the thing works. It is the view of the philosopher Mary Midgley that the failure of science is very much broader than its epistemological failing, but this latter is at the heart of it. Education for the sciences is, she writes:

> An education which trains them in scientific thinking, greatly exaggerates the precision possible to it, while doing very little to teach them the ways of thinking which they will need for other purposes – personal, political, psychological, historical, metaphysical and all the rest.[13]

Julian Huxley long ago attempted to formulate a 'religion without revelation' that would 'restate the realities of spiritual values which my experiences had forced upon me in terms of an intellectual framework drawn from my scientific training,' born of his conviction that 'religion of the highest and fullest character can co-exist with a complete absence of belief in revelation in any straightforward sense of the word, and of belief in that kernel of revealed religion, a personal god.'[14] For Huxley religion is 'a way of life which follows necessarily from a man's holding certain things in reverence, from his feeling and believing them to be sacred. And those things which are held sacred by religion primarily concern human destiny and the forces with which it comes into contact.'

> For my own part, the sense of spiritual relief which comes from rejecting the idea of God as a supernatural being is enormous. I see no other way of bridging the gap between the religious and the scientific approach to reality.
>
> The problem is to make a religion for those men and women, whose numbers are bound to increase with the spread of education, and who will otherwise be left without a religion, or with one to which they cannot whole-heartedly give their assent.[15]

What kind of God?

> Your elephant is an impossible monster, contrary to the laws of
> comparative anatomy, as far as yet known. To which you might
> answer the less, the more you thought.
>
> Charles Kingsley, *The Water Babies*, Chapter 2

The alternative to denial, to abandonment of the concept of God,
is to look again into ourselves and out at the universe in which
we are enfolded and enmeshed, in the new light of all science
has taught us; and ask whether the ultimate reality we have
been trying unsuccessfully to articulate has dimmed or vanished before that dazzling new light – and we may find that the
falling away of the scaffolding, the crutches of outmoded words
and concepts, only reveals it more purely and starkly. Clearly,
all that science has revealed – for revelation in the theological
sense it is – about the nature of the universe, and of the nature of
life and its evolution, requires a radical metamorphosis for
which that process in the life of insects is an appropriate
metaphor.

Although we may have the capacity to understand a little of
how God made the universe, it would be presumptuous beyond
measure to think that we should on this account alone be able to
share in the *why* of it, in God's own acclaim as it were – any more
than the dipper can apprehend our understanding, though perhaps we can imagine that its acclaim echoes the possibility of
what we might be, just as our worship acknowledges an Infinity
beyond our capacity to apprehend.

By the same token, we are not capable of fully understanding
God's action in the world for what it is. There are phenomena
and experiences whose explanation defeats us – the existence of
evil and the suffering of the innocent above all. For some things
there is no answer we can hear with comfort. In spite of our
ages-long search, we can formulate no satisfactory explanation,
because there is none, and if there is no more to it then our reason must rebel; and if in this we are Job reborn then so be it – we
will await our God to lift us onto a plane from which we may see
how this incomprehensible contradiction can be part of the
creation's plan.

But what sort of meaningless language is this? What higher

plane can there be? If we still cling to the shape of things as we experience them there is none. Anyone who comes to rest in the state of denial will be averse to taking this any further, because it is more comfortable and reassuring, less demanding intellectually and emotionally, to remain in that state, and there is every justification for this as being the only choice a truly 'rational' man or woman can make.

A personal God?

Pre-scientific deism or theism is couched in the superstitious language and concepts characteristic of the childhood of our species. Modern atheism is the exhilarating adolescent freedom of discovering there is no Santa Claus. But there is no room for complacency in those of us who can to some extent see this. Our own faith has scarcely begun its moult towards winged maturity out of our former caterpillar selves.

Recognition of a hyper-rational intelligence as the ultimate explanation is not uncommon among philosophers. The deist position represents the simplest version of this. Others go further: various distances along the spectrum of theistic responses, which sees the hand of God still at work within the processes and products of evolution. But the experience of humanity suggests that we should also suspect that the God behind and within all is not only super-rational but super-personal, and it is from this intellectual starting point that we can begin to look for ways in which that super-personal reality may be involved in human history – which is beyond the purview of this book – and in particular in the history of Jews and Christians.

If all our attempts to think or speak of God are so limited by our creatureliness, then our attempts to comprehend or articulate the reality of God's involvement at a personal level in evolution (and not just in the human history of *Homo sapiens*, but of other intelligent human species now extinct) must be equally feeble. Our attempts must take the form of narrative, of history, and being part of this narrative gives us a new meaning and direction, a *telos* comes into focus. Our account of it can only be as it is experienced and interpreted from our side of the veil. What it means within the fullness of meaning on the other side we can have no conception of, except in our awareness that what flowers in us through personhood and reflective awareness as virtue is the merest tinkle of the symphony of which our experience is a faint echo.

And we should remind ourselves that God's personal relationship with sapient humanity is not unique. It may develop on countless other planets, or in other universes, along lines we can only fantasise about.

An awareness of what the presence of God in the human means appears to break through into a new layer of consciousness in Jesus of Nazareth.[16] When it does, there are no words for it. Jesus himself struggles to find them, compelled to reach into the vocabulary of Jewish history and tradition to make anything articulate of who and what he is. How it properly expresses itself is in action, in the living of human life. And this is where Jesus is seen as the Ideal Man – though with all the constraints imposed by his appearance at this particular time in history and of course in this particular culture. The atheist or non-Christian believer can still admire the idealism of the ethic of Jesus: 'the most sublime and benevolent code of morals that has ever been offered to man'.[17] However, most Christian apologists take this, the Great Story, from its beginnings here in first-century Palestine, with a much too easy facility and lack of care for the science and history of things. Within other cultures the awareness of God's presence has taken different forms, with less awareness, or none, that there may be a personal dimension to it.

The life of Jesus of Nazareth shows us the way human beings who are fully responsive to creation would live, except that we as a species are not yet *ready* to live like this. However, the lives of the few who are constitute an essential leaven in society, but when society adopts this way of human living there is the inevitable conflict we see already presaged in the life of Jesus, whose goodness society could not tolerate or take on board, and so he was executed with the barbarity to which human behaviour is still bound.[18]

Many scientific people can accept a deistic interpretation of the universe – there is a creator, but he is remote and impersonal, and does interfere in how things run now, knowing and caring nothing about me as an individual. For Anthony Flew, as for countless sincere explorers in past centuries, this God is not the God of the Bible.[19]

To conceive of our relationship with God as personal – even as the unique relationship of lover and beloved – is however a rational response, but on a level that no ruler or clock can measure the length and breadth and depth of. And being unique both to different cultures and to each individual, it is endlessly varied in the light of individual experience, in degree and depth and with temperament, but the essence of the response is not in the emotion it may give rise to, but in the will, informed by understanding of the world of full experience. On the other hand, we cannot suppose that God's reciprocating love is limited in the way ours is, is of the same 'genus' as that which it reciprocates, as it were. That would be (albeit on an infinitely higher plane) for a loving animal to equate the nature of its master's response with its own. The personhood that looks out at us from the innermost heart of creation is beyond our comprehension, and the loving relationship he hopes for with each of us, unique as is the tinkle of acclaim we can each utter in our love, we can only envision and articulate – and ultimately comprehend – in terms of the behaviour of our embodied person.

From such a reflection we can begin to intimate the worth of every individual person, and the right of each to the opportunity to develop the unique contribution each has to offer. And yet of the 6.5 billion people alive on the planet today, a billion are undernourished, over two million children under the age of five die each year from malnutrition. One person in five has no access to water fit to drink and something like 40 million children are blinded through vitamin A deficiency. A billion live in the slums of teeming cities, and since by 2050 two-thirds of humanity will live in cities (at least a dozen cities will have more than 50 million people each) their numbers will grow and grow. The heroic dedication of Mother Teresa of Calcutta or Abdul Sattar Edhi in Karachi is a defiant translation into action of their belief in the dignity of each individual born into the world. On the other hand, we need to realise with equal clarity that there are too many of us on this earth to live in such a way that each has the opportunity to become all we are capable of, and we must translate that realisation too into the action necessary to ensure that while every human being has what is necessary, we provide it in ways that do not compromise the integrity of the earth's resources and regulatory systems, or its biological diversity. We can only meet this challenge if our lifestyle is shaped by our own deep acceptance of the duty laid upon our individual and collective shoulders in this regard, and if the concept of duty in this context takes on the deeper meaning it must have if our forward movement into history is to be sustainable and not swept up in disaster.

Although they do not find it necessary to bring their quest for the meaning of the world into focus around the word 'God,' Confucians or Buddhists may be no less moral than we Christians are. It may be argued, however, that a contemplation of reality that seeks rather to penetrate to the true essence of things than detachment from them, and that never loses its grounding in reason, will find intimations of relationship and personhood emanating from the depth of that experience – although we know our human grasp of these realities can be no more than a palest reflection or echo of their source.

Growing up: the evolution of belief

We are endowed by our evolutionary unfolding with a physical, biological and psychological endowment that enables us to resonate on a succession of different levels with the harmony of the universe. But we are in need also of a cultural framework within which to find *expression* for it. That can only be what our historical level of attainment allows. The growth of human understanding constantly enlarges the framework. The articulation of divine purpose with which we fill the framework, and which is always straining against the confining bars for a greater adequacy, must expand accordingly, every enlargement an increment in maturity.

When you are confronted by evidence that the faith in which you were brought up no longer provides an adequate explanation for the nature, meaning and purpose of life, you have three choices. You can refuse to accept the evidence and continue as before. You can abandon the faith you grew up with because it has proved to be inadequate. Or you can accept the new knowledge and use it to develop a more mature understanding of what lies at the core of your beliefs. The first response is intellectually dishonest, the second intellectual laziness. But adopting a stance of critical acceptance means a re-interpretation of core concepts that will not be easy for us. It requires the exercise of courage and a plethora of other virtues that have been gathering dust in our spirit – if indeed we have ever had occasion to flex the muscles by which they operate!

Julian Huxley has been one of the most articulate exponents of the need to subject faith and religion to the same rigorous discipline as science. He speaks of the way religion, like all human cultural constructs, must evolve:

> Whereas once it is realised that religious truth is the product of human mind and therefore as incomplete as scientific truth, as partial as artistic expression, the proof or even the suggestion of inadequacy would be welcomed as a means to arriving at a fuller truth and an expression more complete.[20]

But evolution always builds upon what already exists, each species a construct shaped and re-shaped in response to the changing environment over the ages. Religion is exactly the same. And so, just as I cannot jettison my brachiating tree-dwelling ancestors because I don't like the idea of having such a family tree, neither can I abandon my Catholicism or Islam because I have outgrown their retarded intellectual stances. We strive, as best the age we are born into allows us, to conceive, though we know we cannot, the Reality beyond; but with the handing on of the striving of one era to another, that newer conception itself often becomes the reality, rather than the work in endless progress which it is.

We think we really know the story today (because we know it in so much greater detail), but we just as unconsciously, unthinkingly insist on telling it in the same language as before. Every advance in understanding invites us to a deeper faith. For many of us the growth of our scientific understanding shows the inadequacy of the faith we grew up with and so we have at least the courage to abandon it. Fewer of us continue the search, in the knowledge that faith is, ultimately, not a question of yes or no. We must evaluate the achievement of any earlier stage or facet in the development of Christianity in the light of what had gone before, and in the light of the limits of understanding of such earlier stages. The advance of our understanding and achievement is, like natural selection in organic evolution (of which it is a part), slowly incremental.

It is worth reminding ourselves in passing that our 'traditional' understanding is sometimes far removed from what these concepts originally meant at their core. They have often been handed down to us sheathed in shells of outmoded understanding that may altogether smother the kernel that lies at the core, and these layers need to be peeled away at such cost to our comfort that it is tempting to jettison the entire concept and look for a replacement. But it is also important to remember the danger of ill-founded condescension when we are reading the words of earlier explorers of the tradition: people who were among the best minds and souls of their time.

To meet the challenge posed by advances in the modern understanding of reality we will find we need to interpret Christian virtue in a new way: to develop for starters a stronger and richer notion of what fortitude, hope and humility mean, so that they can again shine like the jewels in the crown of our human being-in-the-world they were seen to be in the beginning. To this we will return.

The ultimate questions
> I do not know what is untried and afterward,
> But I know it will in its turn prove sufficient, and cannot fail.
> Walt Whitman, *Song of Myself* 43

And what of such great questions as life eternal and the future of mankind? Will my consciousness survive without me, to merge with some cosmic consciousness, as Hinduism claims; or is it even possible that my individuality could, in some sense inconceivable to us now, continue? Each of us knows himself to be unique and central, and not to be lost. But how our uniqueness may be gathered up in the ultimate folding together of the universe we are incapable of knowing. Whether we can have any faith in it depends ultimately on how we respond to what we encounter in creation.

When we have no tool but the imagination with which our animal soul gifts us (and is so completely tailored to this earth) we can see nothing beyond death but the dark night of timeless darkness. When intellect is our only other tool, meaninglessness is added to this darkness. When we confront and absorb creation within the deeper and wider mode of encounter sketched earlier neither of these responses is adequate. But what we can say is that we will have to look beyond life and being for whatever, if anything, the metaphors of heaven, eternal life, nirvana mean. We have had to abandon belief in heaven, because our concept of heaven is in too direct a line of descent from a geocentric – and anthropocentric – universe. Of course, Islam still maintains such a belief, as Christianity did until recently, but it can only do so through the selective rejection of science that we found in chapter 1 to be inconsistent with the unrestricted application of reason.

What any further state might be we can have no idea of, form no pictures of – but as all we can do is think in pictures (except when we put on the blindfold of mathematics to see beyond) we must fall back on metaphor. Just as there *is* no God – and just as our imagination and intellect are utterly incapable of formulating an adequate concept or 'picture' of God, so too there can be no continuation of *life* as we have lived it, beyond the grave. Our body is designed for this earth. We can have no idea of what, if anything, comes after; to paraphrase St Paul, our sensory experience does not prepare us for it.[21] But if I believe all is in God's hands, then I can accept whatever comes after, because this is the part I am meant to play in the unfolding pattern. And like Hans Küng, I too hope 'not to die into nothingness, which seems to me to be extremely irrational and senseless'.[22]

I think the last word on this can be left to Arthur Peacocke.

[The Judaeo-Christian tradition looks forward] to a stage in cosmic history in which time as we know it will cease and in which God's purposes for the created order and for humanity will be consummated by all being taken up, in some new form, into the divine life. This hope can rest only on what is believed to be the character of God as creative Love and, in my view, can have no other basis. What this consummation (this 'End', *eschaton*, Omega point) might consist in has been the subject of much speculation – including the last book of the New Testament, Revelation. I prefer to be judiciously agnostic about its nature, and to rely entirely on the character of God ... All speculation on detailed scenarios of this consummation, the theological exercise called 'eschatology', surely constitutes a supreme example of attempting to formulate a theory underdetermined by the facts. As such, it seems to me a fruitless and unnecessary exercise – for the source of Christian hope rests only on the steadfastness and faithfulness of the God who is revealed as Love.[23]

I hope when my own time comes I will have the faith, at the heart of what pain or dimming of powers the years will bring, to echo the words of the oceanographer Otto Pettersson, whose love of life and sense of wonder when he faced death at the age of 93 were as great as they had been half a century before. 'What will sustain me in my last moments', he told his son, 'is an infinite curiosity as to what is to follow.'[24]

Disposition

One of the most wonder-inspiring things is the way each of us is unique in personality, each of us with a different contribution to make to the great unfolding of the possibility that the universe holds.

But do we need to add this God dimension? Are we any better for it? And in any case, we must wonder how supremely intelligent people take up such opposite positions on so fundamental a subject as the existence of God. It may be, in fact, that the distance between what seem to be diametrically opposed perspectives is not as great as it first appears, and the difference largely a matter of language and focus. Even Dawkins is prepared to concede that language is at the heart of the matter.[25] The concept of God against which the atheistic 'guru-scientists' (Arthur Peacocke's term) rail is one we are outgrowing, and the tone of the language they use is not designed to support or encourage the slow metamorphosis the process of acquiring new and more mature religious metaphors involves.

But aside from that, those of us who believe in God are surrounded by relatives, friends and acquaintances who do not. These are people who are no worse than we are, no less intelligent – often indeed they may be more than we are on both counts, and sometimes very close to us. What do we have that they do not have; what do we see that is hidden from them? More often than not, what we have and what we see are not what our unbelieving nearest and dearest think we have or see, or think we think we have. For example, I prefer not to have to answer the question 'Do you believe in God?' with a simple Yes or No. But if I just had to answer Yes or No, then the answer is Yes. If the question is 'Would you be prepared to die for your belief?' I would want to answer 'Not if I can help it,' but that presents a multitude of further questions, to only one of which my answer would be Yes, so again if the answer must be Yes or No, then Yes.

We are not necessarily closer to God than they. Indeed, we have already seen the way theology can throw our native intimations out of focus in this regard (see also page 178). The human response that can be seen as 'acclaim' resides in disposition rather than in words, and is often more authentic without words if it finds inherited strings of words unable to contain a more mature understanding and cannot find a verbal substitute. But while we may share the same disposition, those of us who profess faith are looking, we would presume to say, in the right direction, and committed to the journey towards the destination to which it leads. We have the conviction that humanity must move in this direction, individually and collectively, equipped with the armoury of reason and virtue. Yet those who do not profess faith may be moving in the same direction, faster than us indeed – it is all too easy to be Pharisees in this regard.

The Trinity

This is the realm of mystery. Of course there is nothing mysterious about it at all, we just don't understand it. The operation of God's personhood is in a realm of mystery that has exercised the Christian imagination and intellect from the earliest days of theology. There is no theology as such in the scriptures, but there is this attempt to grapple with personality in God that eventually crystallised in the notion that it is somehow three-fold: God is Father/Mother, Son/Daughter, and Indwelling Spirit. However, the edifice of Trinitarian theology that has grown around this core notion over the two millennia of

Christianity is so thoroughly infused with the mortar of out-moded cosmology that it cannot but collapse as that cosmology dissolves. If we look to see what new interpretation we can put on that core concept in our day, we can see the Holy Spirit in the inherent potential within the matter of the Singularity to evolve ever higher levels of consciousness in successive embodiments. The Son is actual embodiment at successive levels of God's *verbum*, culminating in the embodiment in the human personhood of Jesus Christ. God the Father is the One who utters the word. On some such basis we may construct a Trinitarian theology more in harmony with our modern understanding of cosmology and evolution: aware that this new construct must itself give way in time, and time again, as our understanding of God evolves and grows.

'A reasonable goal for the cosmic evolutionary purpose?'
Or: are we heading anywhere?

> There is divine chaos, and, in it, limitless hope and possibilities.
> Richard Jefferies, *The Old House at Coate*[26]

The evolutionary unfolding of the possibility inherent in matter has come this far in 14 billion years. Is this its ultimate achievement – apart from continuation of natural selection in a world whose biological diversity is being abused and extinguished on the horrific scale we see all around us? This is where Teilhard is at his most innovative, and it is where he is at his most vulnerable because he is a first explorer in uncharted linguistic territory, groping for words.[27] The angry tone of Sir Peter Medawar's criticism of Teilhard is very reminiscent of Dawkins' tone. Medawar read and studied *The Phenomenon of Man* 'with real distress, even despair, lamenting the 'gullibility that makes it possible for people to be taken in by such a bag of tricks as this'.[28] Jacques Monod's *Chance and Necessity* – although an undoubted classic of modern biology,[29] is also scathing of Teilhard's work to the point of being scurrilous – indeed, slanderous:

> Although Teilhard's logic is hazy and his style laborious, some of those who do not entirely accept his ideology yet allow it a certain poetic grandeur. For my part I am most of

all struck by the intellectual spinelessness of the philosophy. In it I see more than anything else a systematic truckling, a willingness to conciliate at any price, to come to any compromise. Perhaps, after all, Teilhard was not for nothing a member of that order which, three centuries earlier, Pascal assailed for its theological laxness.

But if we are touched by hope, another of the great virtues that consideration of these issues in the light of all our new insights causes to flame to new relevance in our time, then we may feel that other dimensions remain inherent in creation, as yet only *in potentia*, and that humanity is the leading edge of its trajectory. But it would be as impossible for us to attempt to imagine what that might be as for an outside observer to predict life from the laws of inorganic chemistry in the mind game we played earlier.

Increasingly this reach into future is seen as the narrative of our time, both in science and theology: reaching towards a future that holds the promise of fuller being. John Haught identifies with Teilhard here in postulating the future as a power that draws evolution to it rather than a reach implied in the progressive realisation of inherent potentiality.[30] 'The narrative of our day is not about having fallen from a perfect state, but about the endless search for a perfect state somewhere in the future.' That future, we need to remind ourselves, is potentially a very long one: tens of thousands, indeed millions, of years. The Teilhardian articulation will in the course of that time doubtless be abandoned for the inadequacy of the metaphor that it is, just as earlier and now outmoded metaphors of heaven and life eternal are seen as vessels unable to hold the more mature understanding of our time, unable to contain the ultimate meaning the words intend. Just as does science, theology depicts reality 'in metaphorical language with the use of models, and ... their metaphors and models are revisable within the context of the continuous communities which have generated them'.[31] Between the Alpha of our origins and the Omega of our final destination, we may perhaps still have to traverse and decipher most of the letters in the alphabet of human possibility – and it is not necessarily pre-determined that we will ever reach that destination.

Perhaps we can leave the last word to a visionary of a different sort, H. G. Wells (1866-1946), a contemporary of Teilhard, best known for the classic science novels in which he sketched a future many of his contemporaries regarded as purest fantasy. In 1902 Wells wrote an article in the leading science journal *Nature* in which he sketched his vision of the future of mankind. Teilhard was in Jersey at this time; it is possible he read this piece and that it subconsciously influenced his thinking.

It is possible to believe that all the past is but the beginning of a beginning, and that all that is and has been is but the twilight of the dawn. It is possible to believe that all that the human mind has ever accomplished is but the dream before the awakening. We cannot see, there is no need for us to see, what this world will be like when the day has fully come. We are creatures of the twilight. But it is out of our race and lineage that minds will spring, that will reach back to us in our littleness to know us better than we know ourselves, and that will reach forward fearlessly to comprehend this future that defeats our eyes. All this world is heavy with the promise of greater things, and a day will come, one day in the unending succession of days, when beings, beings who are now latent in our thoughts and hidden in our loins, shall stand upon this earth as one stands upon a footstool, and shall laugh and reach out their hands amidst the stars.[32]

CHAPTER NINE

Human ACCLAIM: Virtue and community

> When the world was in darkness and wretchedness, it could be-
> lieve in perfection and yearn for it. But when the world became
> bright with reason and riches, it began to sense the narrowness
> of the needle's eye, and that rankled for a world no longer will-
> ing to believe or yearn.
>
> *A Canticle for Leibowitz*[1]

That the most deeply rational explanation of creation grounds belief in an Ultimate Reality we call God is not a conclusion that will meet with easy acceptance from people with a different perspective – who are most unlikely to be reading this in any case, or who would consider that a book with a title such as this bears might have anything worthwhile to say. Why, then, don't we all respond with acclaim to the deep encounter with creation? In part, of course, for reasons discussed in chapter 8, and in particular the impossibility of reconciling evil and pain with an all-good and all-powerful deity. But that, in fact, is a separate question, and one believers have to contend with more intensely than atheists.

And then, we respond differently because we are differently endowed with the capacity for it, just as we are differently endowed with intellectual capacity in the narrow sense. In part also because the extent or depth of our confrontation with reality is limited by circumstances beyond our control, or because we have become conditioned or grown accustomed to a lesser encounter. We are straying into deeper theological waters here, which a standard treatise on these matters might discuss under the heading of *grace and salvation*. In an earlier Christian theology this dilemma was covered with the concepts of election and predestination, a solution that neatly slipped the noose of the challenge the question poses. In a more conventional treatment a believer might want to say that what is missing in the unbelieving reader is faith. Faith is a gift of God; you have it or you don't. You can do nothing of yourself to win it. I suppose reincarnation can be thought of as another attempt to tackle this dilemma, which remains as great a problem in theology as it ever was. In passing we should note that conversion is a common theme in the web of human experience and human evolution.

There are different levels of acclaim. There is the dipper's acclaim, the acclaim of the spider, of the rose: all different colours in the kaleidoscope of acclaim. And this symphony of acclaim, for all its rising harmony through the evolutionary processes operating over geological time, has its origin in one note, the ultimate OM. What then of the note that is the human acclaim? If creation is as we discover it to be through deep encounter, a response is required of us that reflects the capacities that set us apart from the rest of creation: 'conscious thought, self-consciousness, communication of abstract thoughts to other human beings, the interrelations of personal life and ethical behaviour, creativity in art and science, the apprehension of values – and all that characterises and differentiates humanity from the rest of the biological world'.[2]

First of all it calls us to use those unique qualities to develop a deeper appreciation of the universe God has created, and in particular a more attentive and responsive attitude to the living world, not in order to continue to exploit it for our ends on an ever-increasing scale and with ever-increasing sophistication, which is our main reason for 'doing science' at present, but in order to share more fully, as far as the limits of human-being-in-the-world allow, the efflorescence of Ultimate Being embodied in the material creation. 'Science can only be created by those who are thoroughly imbued with the aspiration towards truth and understanding. The source of this feeling, however, springs from the sphere of religion.'[3]

Apart from the contemplation it calls us to in our individual lives, this deeper attention to creation calls for behavioural change, change in our relationship with the earth, with other people, and with our more distant cousins further back on the Tree of Life. We do not need the tools and insights provided by modern science in order to nurture and develop this growing appreciation in ourselves – but they are a powerful help. It is so very much easier for example to develop an interest in particular facets of the living world when there is such a rich and accessible literature available, and where the media of television and the internet bring the resources of library and screen into our homes. The capacity to respond to the beauty and complexity of creation, to hear and be responsive to the sensory and intellectual symphony of it all, is *instinct* in us. We can often hear this in the writings of those talented with the capacity to find words for it (Thomas Traherne in the 17th century for example), but the less articulate appreciation of the illiterate peasant may be no less intense.

> The WORLD is unknown, till the Value and Glory of it is seen: till the Beauty and the Serviceableness of its parts is considered. When you enter into it, it is an illimited field of Variety and Beauty: where you may lose yourself in the multitude of Wonders and Delights. But it is an happy loss to lose oneself in admiration at one's own Felicity: and to find GOD in exchange for oneself: Which we then do when we see Him in His Gifts, and adore His Glory.
> Your enjoyment of the world is never right, till every morning you awake in Heaven; see yourself in your Father's Palace; and look upon the skies, the earth, and the air as Celestial Joys: having such a reverend esteem of all, as if you were among the Angels.[4]

The living earth is the very womb within which and out of which we have evolved. Contemplation of its wonder provides our first glimpse of the beauty and goodness of the divine, and is the fount of that concern which has matured over time to include an ethics of responsibility for creation. Over this last century in particular we have seen the diminution of the living diversity of that creation and of the health of the ecosystems that support it.[5] At no time in human history has it been more difficult to experience the natural world as it is meant to be experienced, because of the way contemporary human living abuses and smothers it. We are responsible for compromising the integrity of life's regulatory systems and the profligate use of its mineral resources. We are responsible for the way precious soil is stripped by erosion from the surface of the earth,[6] for the unsustainable use of its water.[7] We use our brains to force the living creation to retreat further and further from us in spatial terms, with consequences for the balance of the earth and for ourselves that we can as yet barely glimpse, and in the process we are responsible for the fading of colour from the earth's rainbow of biodiversity.[8] No longer can each of us stand before the living world as Adam called to encounter each creature by name, no longer alone and unique before God in this special way: 'By making one, and not a multitude, God evidently shewed one alone to be the end of the World and every one its enjoyer. For every one may enjoy it as much as he.'[10] Every second of every day an area of rainforest the size of a football field falls to fire and chainsaw, adding its smoke to the brown pall that dims the light of the sun and poisons the air.

Is the acclaim that is asked of us, then, different in kind? Indeed yes, for we are called to be children of God in a new sense never before seen on earth – for all of life's wondrous and diverse achievement. To us alone it has been given to appreciate God's plan on the level of understanding. But we are fully human only in community. Nothing is more important to individual integrity and self-worth than a sense of belonging, which is why the creation, repair and development of community are a central concern of all modern societies.[11]

Virtue

> At the least, an awareness of cosmic evolution aims us, indeed like an arrow, toward an Ethical Epoch as a firm prerequisite for our future well-being. ... Perhaps we are now on the path toward ethical evolution, arguably part of a cosmological imperative to help us address the many varied challenges along the future arrow of time.
>
> Eric Chaisson, *Epic of Evolution: Seven Ages of the Cosmos*

Telos is the overarching purpose of human life – of my individual life, the life of the community, of the human species, and of life on earth. In the absence of God we are stumbling blindly through history into nothingness, and there is nothing to strive for that is worth the effort of all our energies at the task of realising ourselves, each to the best of his or her ability. But if there is a Mind at work in the unfolding and deepening of Meaning in the universe, albeit a Mind whose understanding at times bewilders mine, then I will want to live on this earth in the way that constitutes an appropriate response to the God who speaks wordlessly to me out of the depth of my sensory encounter with reality. The appropriate human response, very broadly conceived, is the virtuous life, some aspects of which we have lightly touched upon earlier.

We will in due course be called to account, because we appear unable to call ourselves to account, incapable as we seem to be of acting collectively with the same intelligence and integrity we can embody as individuals and in community. But in the longer term it may be through cultivating in ourselves and in our communities the qualities and capacities of attitude and behaviour appropriate to human acclaim that we will make our best contribution to the human future and the future of earth. We can translate that to mean a life that is governed by virtue: the cultivation within ourselves of those qualities of character that reason and reflection show to be necessary for the caring of the earth, the survival and continued progress of humanity, and the fulfillment of our individual destiny. For Thomas Aquinas virtue was *ultimum potentiae*: the absolute best we are capable of as human beings.

This is using language that has gone out of fashion. Virtue is not usually used as a measure of progress or happiness. Progress in our culture of unlimited access to material goods is measured by criteria that rely heavily on words like growth and upgrade, but growth in this sense means growth in economic terms, determined by such measures as GDP, and upgrade is technological upgrade, whereas what the world needs most now, as it has always done, is growth and upgrade in the human qualities to which that apparently outmoded concept of virtue refers.

We have come to think of virtue as something to be found in people who are 'holy': but the concept goes much deeper than this. Virtue is the disposition and behaviour appropriate to what human being is supposed to be. It is living life as we should live it by virtue of who and what we are meant to be; and in earlier chapters we have tried to focus on what this might be in the light of creation and the unfolding of intelligence within life. Virtue is what we are called to, if you like. It is what we must wear if we are to travel the right path in life,[12] even if it doesn't appear to provide us with signposts to where we are headed. It is for soldiers, politicians, bricklayers and taxi drivers as much as for nuns, priests, mullahs and atheists. The search for it is at the very heart of western philosophy, is indeed what it is all about, from Socrates, Plato and Aristotle to its florid elaboration in medieval scholasticism, then on through the minefield of re-interpretation that is post-Enlightenment philosophy, right down to our own day, where the beauty and dignity of it are all but drowned in the all-encompassing materialism of the modern world.

But now that we have abandoned the notion of a God who will punish us with hell fire eternal for our misdeeds during life, and at the same time no longer entertain the notion of an eternal reward after death with goods our human imaginations can comprehend (see page 138), why bother to be virtuous? Is it possible to retain *absolutes* – things that can take hold of your life and for which you would be prepared to sacrifice all if called upon – *in extremis* even your life – even though they are embodied in an earlier formulation we can no longer accept as adequate? Does the concept of virtue not melt away with the abandonment of the outmoded vessels of language and custom in which it has been carried and transmitted up to now? Organised religion concentrates on the progressive elaboration of these vessels, often to the neglect of the precious essence within. When with the passage of time the flame grows dim in later transmission of the essential vision at the heart of it all, the incidental cultural trimmings take over. There is a need to constantly re-kindle the fire from the embers, in every age, never more urgently than in our own. We may find also that the pure embrace of virtue opens the possibility of common cause with the equally 'disinterested' embrace of humanist and atheist.

As Voltaire so concisely expressed it, *Dans la contrainte point de vertu, et sans vertu point de religion* (Under coercion there is no virtue, and without virtue there is no religion).[13] Virtue is practised for its own sake; it has nothing to do with reward. But what the death of that God with his promises and threats has done is burn away the patina that has accumulated over the virtues with the passage of centuries since the magisterial elaboration of Thomas Aquinas in the 13th century, building on the earlier insights of Aristotle. Virtue is the multi-faceted jewel that illumin-ates our human life from its core; but a new courage is required of us that it may glow in the dark of the world we have made, courage that burns away the pride, superstition and weakness with which its lustre has become obscured. Or if human virtue is a tree, this courage is the pruning of dead and superfluous growth, so that it may flower and bear fruit in season, fruit perhaps it has never been seen or known to bear in our life and times.

Faith

In the traditional classification developed in the Middle Ages there are three theological virtues underpinning Christian belief (faith, hope and charity), and four cardinal virtues upon which Christian living hinges (*cardo* in Latin means a hinge): prudence, justice, courage and temperance. But 'faith' has come to mean many things. There is, at one end of its spectrum of meaning, 'The Faith' with its great panoply of doctrine and dogma, ritual and liturgy, commandments and prohibitions as to how we should and should not behave. But what is the faith for me may not be your faith: religious denominations and creeds are legion. To get at what the simple, unadorned virtue of faith means we need to strip all of this away in order to reach the living kernel at the centre, the thing that is common to all humans. This is the belief that *creation is meant*: that it is within the embrace of an all-encompassing Power from which the beauty, intelligibility and goodness we see reflected in created things radiates. In this essential sense it is the first note of the human acclaim before creation, a note that needs no words: a lowest common denomin-ator of our response, as it were, to be found in every culture and in every age. But having voiced that first note in the human ac-claim of God, how does the song go on? It moves into the realm of concept and word. It can be sung in a thousand, in ten thou-sand ways, constituting a diversity of ritual form that reflects the adaptive radiation of humankind, a radiation that resulted in the linguistic and cultural diversity that has been the crowning achievement of humanity; and this evolves as we evolve, be-coming richer and more elaborate with time.

The efflorescence of liturgy is largely a cultural thing, but its roots are deeper and more essentially human. These roots find expression in the simplest of things – gestures, sounds. Human arms held out, palms upturned, mean more than the mere words of any offertory prayer. Where words are to be added, they can only be metaphor. The problem with 'religion' is that the depth and simplicity of that 'primitive' response becomes encrusted with layer after layer of theological elaboration, becoming so deep over time that the heartbeat within is stilled, the awe dulled, the thrill silenced.

But as the kernel of our response begins to germinate in response to our inevitable questioning about the kind of Power this is, and about the implications it holds for our behaviour, it becomes differentiated and acquires layer after layer of overlay that obscures and perhaps ultimately stifles the seed at the heart of the lustrous pearl it becomes with time. Whatever our individual cultural and religious heritage, we need to be able to peel away that overlay and recover that seed in our own lives.

Faith is our essential response to what is being 'said' to us in creation, and it is the radical dividing line in human attitude towards the cosmos. It arises, therefore, out of our experience of the creation, but that experience is endlessly varied. The more deeply we become immersed in it, the more cogently beauty, intelligence and goodness impose themselves upon our minds, and the more feeble and inadequately rational a negative response appears. Faith is a disposition that is born of, follows from, the deeper mode of encounter with creation, what Hans Küng calls 'a radical rationality'.[14] The 'scientific' encounter, in the generally accepted sense of seeking and finding intelligible explanations for the *how of things*, is a lesser and more partial experience. Faith arises from the capacity to see the holism hiding at the very deepest level of reality, to know that the most truly rational response to creation is Yes. It is before and beyond proof. If it either needed proof or could be proved scientifically it would not be faith. In itself it is ineffable, but once it begins to clothe itself (as it must) in the culturally determined attire of language and ritual it becomes differentiated, a Tower of Babel, and religion crystallises out of it. Great minds have down the ages built castles of rationalisation and theologising upon a foundation of limited experience. Such towers and castles come tumbling down when we allow ourselves to be immersed more deeply in the reality of things.

It is the intelligibility that suffuses all things that makes possible the encounter of which the investigations of science are the first level. And it is essentially the beauty that these investigations reveal to us that is the motivating force of science. To what uses we should put our greater understanding is a later question. 'The scientist does not study nature because it is useful; he studies it because he delights in it, and he delights in it because it is beautiful.'[15]

What faith requires of us is an openness to God similar to that outlined in a famous letter from (of all people!) Thomas Huxley to Charles Kingsley:

> Science seems to me to teach in the highest and strongest manner the great truth which is embodied in the Christian conception of entire surrender to the will of God. Sit down before fact as a little child, be prepared to give up every preconceived notion, follow humbly wherever and to whatever abysses Nature leads, or you shall learn nothing. I have only begun to learn content and peace of mind since I resolved at all risks to do this.[16]

This expresses an attitude that is little different from that wonderful prayer composed by Archbishop Fenelon, which expresses, I feel, the embrace of the world that this new faith and the hope that accompanies it arise out of. It is a prayer of its age, as all prayer and every expression of faith must be, inadequate, in need of re-formulation as soon as it leaves our lips. It rises up not out of the mainstream of Catholic thought in the early 18th century, but in a side stream that wandered in search of a deeper vision (the Quietist movement of the time).

> Lord, I know not what I ought to ask of Thee; Thou only knowest what I need; Thou lovest me better than I know how to love myself. O Father, give to Thy child that which he himself knows not how to ask. I dare not ask either for crosses or for consolations; I simply present myself before Thee, I open my heart to Thee. Behold my needs which I know not myself; see and do according to Thy tender mercy. Smite, or heal; depress me, or raise me up; I adore all Thy purposes without knowing them; I am silent; I offer myself in sacrifice; I yield

myself to Thee; would have no other desire than to accomplish Thy will. Teach me to pray. Pray Thyself in me. Amen.[17]

Hope

The Christian thinker must risk his own soul for each answer. And even then he does not know whether his answer is the correct one. His mute prayer always continues to be, 'Lord, I believe, help my unbelief.'
We have also to consider that God has only revealed sufficient for us to be able to risk the next step towards him in hope, into the darkness, trusting that his light will continue to shine for us.

Ladislaus Boros[18]

Faith generates the optimism that, just as there is something behind the meaning of things that goes far beyond the explanation of how it works, so too, more than mere extinction stands beyond life and the end of time. This is the virtue of hope. Of course we can have no knowledge whatever of what that means. Seeing, as we do on this earth, 'through a glass, darkly,' 'eye hath not seen, nor ear heard, neither hath it entered into the heart of man, what things God hath prepared for them that love him.'[19] It would not be hope if it were based on knowledge, which is concerned only with the operation of matter and energy in this universe. What you have when you already know beforehand what Santa will bring you on Christmas morning is not hope.

My trust in God's own *telos* is deep enough to accept in advance, without knowing, whatever lies ahead of me, even beyond death, as that which is in best harmony with the direction of the universe's own becoming. Knowing that final letting go of life as I comprehend life will involve change beyond comprehension, I cannot but be apprehensive and fearful. Yet even if I do fall, my God, I know my fall will metamorphose into flight, even when that flight takes me where I cannot follow.

Charity

There is in us a world of Love to somewhat, though we know not what in the world that should be.

Thomas Traherne, *Centuries of Meditations* I, 2

Those whose lives are fired by faith and hope find in themselves an attitude towards other selves that evokes sympathy, compassion, a sense of being bonded. There is no satisfactory word for this, although the thoughtful formulators of antiquity called it charity and made it the third theological virtue. 'Charity' is the word used in older English translations of the New Testament for the Latin *caritas*, which was St Jerome's rendering of the original Greek *agapé*. Martin Luther preferred 'love' to 'charity', and indeed in modern translations such as the New English Bible 'charity' is replaced by 'love'. The problem is that both of these words mean something quite different from what *agapé* is trying to convey. Part of the difficulty comes from the fact that it is a new word, newly minted to convey the new dispensation of the followers of Jesus. Over and over – 21 times – the word appears in the New Testament, but never in the Old Testament. St Paul goes to great pains in his first letter to the Christians of Corinth to explain what the word means, precisely because there was no familiar word to equate with it – not altogether successfully, because it is so much more than a mere word. It condenses to a single word what Jesus had already encapsulated in a sentence as the second of the two great commandments: 'love other people the way you love yourself.' What is this *agapé* but the recognition of myself in the countenance of every other human being, an acknowledgement not merely of the blood ties that bind us all in brotherhood, but that you are me?

> If I speak in the tongues of mortals and of angels, but do not have love, I am a noisy gong or a clanging cymbal. And if I have prophetic powers, and understand all mysteries and all knowledge, and if I have all faith, so as to remove mountains, but do not have love, I am nothing. If I give away all my possessions, and if I hand over my body so that I may boast, but do not have love, I gain nothing. Love is patient; love is kind; love is not envious or boastful or arrogant or rude. It does not insist on its own way; it is not irritable or resentful; it does not rejoice in wrongdoing, but rejoices in the truth. It bears all things, believes all things, hopes all things, endures all things. Love never ends. But as for prophecies, they will come to an end; as for tongues, they will cease; as for knowl-

edge, it will come to an end. For we know only in part, and we prophesy only in part; but when the complete comes, the partial will come to an end. When I was a child, I spoke like a child, I thought like a child, I reasoned like a child; when I became an adult, I put an end to childish ways. For now we see in a mirror, dimly, but then we will see face to face. Now I know only in part; then I will know fully, even as I have been fully known. And now faith, hope, and love abide, these three; and the greatest of these is love.[20]

This love is expressed most easily and naturally with those who are closest to us, most a part of us; it is the fountainhead of human ethics, but the widening of the ripples of human consanguinity elevates our concern onto a new level entirely (see page 93).

In this virtue of charity lies the salvation of the world. Only if we are prepared to love in the way laid down by Jesus of Nazareth can humanity achieve its potential: a prescription that echoes the teaching of all the other great religious figures who came before and those who have followed him in history. We must cultivate in ourselves the awareness that every human being sees himself at the centre of everything that happens, just as I do. I must strive to accord to each the consideration and regard I would wish for myself. I can practise faith and hope in the isolation of my home or in church, but what I think or say or do there counts for nothing on their own. It is my behaviour that shows what I am really made of. Charity is the way I behave in the street, in the marketplace, in my work. It is how I behave in response to what faith and hope have awakened in me. With the loss of faith, charity fades to the philanthropy necessary for economic and political stability.

This is the essence of being a Christian, the second of the two great commandments by which our behaviour is to be guided if our thought and reflection are really true to what creation reveals. The first commandment, as Jesus understood it, is to have the virtue of faith: 'Thou shalt love the Lord thy God with all thy heart, and with all thy soul, and with all thy mind. This is the first and great commandment. And the second is like unto it, Thou shalt love thy neighbour as thyself. On these two commandments hang all the law and the prophets.'[21]

Paul's lengthy commentary shows how difficult it is to contain in a word what can really only be described by a life. That is what he is trying to do in a generalised sort of way, but it is more immediately understandable by pointing to the individual lives of people who try to live by this rule: Albert Schweitzer, Teresa of Calcutta, Damien of Molokai, countless missionary men and women of all denominations, and all the others you can add to the list, some of whom you know personally. You will not number yourself among them because humility enables you to know better, and indeed stones can be hurled at anyone on the list once you forget that our attempt to live a life infused and directed by this *agapé* is accompanied by the knowledge and acceptance of our own failure to live up to it. It will not be easy, because the society in which we live no longer lights its way towards the future by this guiding light. This does not mean I must shun the world, turn my back on it. But it calls for greater sympathy, subtlety and intelligence in the way I integrate myself if I am to bring the little spark of my influence to bear: 'Behold I send you as sheep in the midst of wolves. Be ye therefore wise as serpents and simple as doves.'[22]

Those of us who believe in God – and I hope we are sufficiently advanced in our discussion now to permit tentative use of this metaphor – find faith, hope and charity lightly brushing the fringes of lives dominated by more urgent, day-to-day concerns. There are also those select ones among us who are so imbued, so blown away with the power and penetration of these virtues that their lives are a beacon to all whose lives they touch.

The cardinal virtues

It is in community, in particular, that the need for us to exercise the cardinal virtues is most clearly in evidence, and although that exercise is central for society in any geographical or cultural context in order to function well, it takes on a new urgency in the face of the social and environmental challenges we confront in our time. Overpopulation, and the strain this places on the earth's limited resources gives added urgency to the need for justice and temperance. What is required of us as a species, as communities and as individuals, if we are to come to terms with climate change and resource depletion, places unprecedented urgency on the need for prudence, justice and temperance. And we need to find a new fortitude to counter the temptation to complacency, ennui or despair. The problems we face are too great for despair to be an option. And for our affluent corner of the world, the virtue of temperance is a beacon in the gathering fog.

Temperance introduces the notion of discipline and self-sacrifice, which lose their meaning when they are disconnected from their ends. We read of the penitential practices of an earlier age with amazement – the nettle bath of brave Willie Doyle and Matt Talbot's vest of chains spring to mind as familiar 20th-century examples. Such practice is outmoded, but what lies at the heart of it is not. And the danger is that revulsion at the fashion of a bygone era drowns that essential thing. The purpose of discipline is to keep our mind, body and spirit at their most alert, so that we can be the best we are capable of being, keeping our lamps trimmed and in readiness, if you like, for when their light will be needed.[23]

It is about keeping fit, really, in the broadest sense: our bodies being, after all, 'temples of the holy ghost'. George Sheehan went out running each day, even in his seventies, as he counted down the weeks to the end of his life, 'to preserve the self I attained the day before. And coupled with this is the desire to secure the self yet to be. There can be no let up.'[24] This is meaningful discipline. By way of contrast, the discipline of an earlier age was disconnected from its end. Earlier embodiments of the notion of sacrifice are outmoded. To sacrifice means (literally) to make holy. We make our lives holy through virtue, the exercise of which requires discipline of us. In a more primitive age sacrifice was equated with the taking of life rather than the living of life. Outmoded though our Age of Reason has made it, we still preserve this language in our liturgy.

The virtue of humility

As these defining qualities of human character grow within us over the course of our individual lives, other virtues take root in us. Academic theology has devised a much more elaborate taxonomy of virtue than this of course,[25] but a more extended and adequate account would require a volume all to itself. Virtue is all of a piece, of course, each quality linked to others, and every one of us has the call and capacity to develop a different spectrum, unique to each person. One further virtue needs to be mentioned here, however, for one thing because it is so misinterpreted, and for another because of its relevance to our theme. Humility is usually thought of as a virtue of the weak, requiring deference, taking the lowest place, thinking little of ourselves. And it is, indeed, about knowing our place. It accepts the absolute groundedness of our biological belonging to this earth and nowhere else (no*where* else). It moves us to compassion for all who share that kinship and belonging. It acknowledges the limitations of the human capacity to know, for all its god-like qualities, and the provisionality of all paradigms.

* * *

Virtue must be balanced in the individual. It's not enough to be brilliant at one thing, brilliant hurler or mathematician, however exemplary *per se* for others striving to perfect that virtue. The all-virtuous man or woman is a blueprint, not a real creature of flesh and blood. And there is a lifetime's striving in trying to get closer to it. But there is great wisdom in Alexander Pope's 'To err is human, to forgive divine,' so that forgiveness is infinite, but so too the striving that is the pilgrim's journey of our lives must be a progress, and our effort at virtue (as at forgiveness) seventy times seven.[26]

The evangelical counsels

What are called the evangelical counsels of perfection (poverty, chastity, obedience) must also be brought within the compass of the constellation of virtues that need to characterise a truly rational and responsive human life. These are the vows that people in 'religious life' take: but have they not now had their day? Or if they are to be relevant, surely it can only be in some watered-down and minimalist re-interpretation? No indeed, for they have never been more relevant. But what is needed is a more essential interpretation. Poverty is not wanting more than I need to fulfill my role in life. It is knowing when I have enough. It is a respect for the things of creation, so that it abhors waste and the abuse of material goods. Chastity is the disposition that puts love before everything else, in the sense of treating all other persons I relate to with the care and concern I have for myself. Obedience is the determination to lead my life in accordance with the blueprint for human behaviour that comes into focus from deep experience and encounter with creation. Interestingly, in the Orthodox tradition a fourth vow is added: stability (fidelity to one place: see page 166).

* * *

This need for human practice to continually moult in order to keep abreast of evolving society so that it may continue to mould and guide it is not confined to the practice of virtue. It bears equally on the need for theology and liturgy to do likewise, and the lag here is greater even than it is in relation to virtue. That axiom of the early Church Fathers, *ecclesia semper reformanda*, is perhaps more relevant in our time than it has ever been. That discussion must await another day and a different forum, however. Bernard Lonergan's famous remark that the church inevitably arrives on the scene of the action 'late and a little out of breath' is perhaps over-generous in terms of time.[27] Gabriel Moran once wrote of 'the need for a theological method far wider than that provided by the older Word of God or the newer hermeneutical theologies of the continent of Europe' in the age of the earth in which we live.[28] We can be distracted from the need for the radical reform of liturgy our New Age calls for by the geographically staggered nature of development, which allows an outmoded theology to thrive where concerns that bear more urgently on the needs of everyday life are uppermost.

Virtue, telos and community

The *acquisition* of virtue is a life-long process of learning, discipline and purification. The *practice* of virtue requires a shared *telos* within a community.[29] At many times throughout history, and in many cultures, the individual *telos* has been that of the community and of society as a whole, but such a society falters and ultimately fails when reason becomes corrupted or virtue fails – or both. But with the loss of a *telos* that is grounded in that ultimate reality whose nature we feebly explored earlier, society is headless, and without belief in an ultimate purpose for its activity, essentially rudderless because it has no instinct for where it may be going.[30] Such collapse is often precipitated by environmental change to which reason and virtue could have provided solutions, had reason been adequately developed and virtue sufficiently diffused within the society, because human reason is the ultimate anchor for human progress and virtue its driving force.

The unique achievement of late medieval Europe was the re-establishment of reason at the heart of the enterprise of seeking, finding and living for, with and in God, with the potential to blossom as a society founded on reason and virtue following on from the re-discovery and further development of Aristotle's articulation of a rational approach and response to what creation is saying to us. But the medieval achievement was as embryonic as it was precarious, and the level of admiration in our own restrospective evaluation is likely to be limited if we fail to appreciate the possibilities that might have been realised had it endured long enough for that embryo to develop. As it is, the intellectual brilliance of medieval philosophy is profoundly obscured from our view by the stultifying formulaic language of Scholasticism, so much of which is an exercise in mental gymnastics that flexed intellectual muscles of little relevance in running the race of everyday human life, and which is moreover articulated (with unquestioning confidence) against a cosmological background we know to be wrong.

At the heart of the Enlightenment philosophy that succeeded the Medieval Synthesis lay the newly conceived conviction that we can explain the workings of the world without recourse to God's direct intervention (so pithily summed up in Laplace's *je ne pas besoin de cette hypothese* – I don't need God to explain it). By Kant's time the scope of reason had narrowed to the 'reduction of the radius of science and reason' to which Benedict XVI refers,[31] and so whereas Christianity continues to insist on the unity of reason and faith, Kant and other Enlightenment philosophers concluded that they were different, and that reason has to be set to one side when we talk about faith, and about ethics.

And although for most of the brilliant minds involved, God was still the Great Architect behind it all and creation continued to be thought of as his handiwork, he was now an all-powerful and ingenious mechanic rather than a magician. But with this new perspective it became possible to decouple God from creation. If it is unnecessary to invoke God's direct action in order to explain the clockwork of the universe, why then there's no need for God at all! Whereas in fact, all that could really be claimed was that reason was capable of understanding (superficially at least) *how* it works.

For all the progress and material gain we have derived from the advance of science and technology, the loss of overarching purpose has been a canker at the heart of the legacy of the Enlightenment. This came about on the one hand (on the secular front) because of the failure of the new naturalists to reach deeply enough into the well of reality to develop the more mature articulation of the notion of God that would allow 'faith' to continue to be rational; but on the other hand (on the ecclesiastical side, and in spite of the insistence referred to above) the cutting loose of reason in this way freed religion from the need to fully embrace the deeper understanding of creation that the growth of science presented it with, because of the fear of moving out of the theological and political comfort zone of what had already been achieved, complacent in the conviction that it had a written revelation that took priority as a source of truth. In this way, 'by their failure over science and new developments in philosophy, society, and politics, theology and the church essentially contributed to the establishment of scientific and political atheism.'[32]

But it is only when the *telos* that sees God as its goal and motivation is restored as society's overarching goal that human life can be lived to the full, and at its most deeply rational. And it is only in that embrace that the individual life recovers its true dignity and harnesses its true capacity. In the meantime, each of us must work as best our capacity allows us, to correct the dysfunctionality induced in our individual lives by our failure in virtue and reason: and this is best done from within the community into which we have been born and grown up, however greatly in need of correction that Communion of Saints and Sinners may be, and however many millennia of erratic progress it takes to effect that metamorphosis.

Personality

Thus, while we wait in hope for a recovery of *telos* within the broader society, which may take centuries or millennia, we are called upon to sustain it within community, and in particular within the natural community that finds its cultural and spiritual correlative in the parish, as well as within the communities of intent where those who feel more passionately called to serve the realisation of the human *telos* gather in solidarity.

One of the most wonder-inspiring things is the way each of us is unique in personality, each with a different contribution to make to the great unfolding of the possibility that the universe holds. In a manner analogous to the way each species is unique, occupying a different corner in creation, a unique realisation of the possibility inherent in matter from the very beginning, so each person is unique, turning an eye and mind on creation that nobody else can turn, with a personality capable of a contribution to the progress of nature and of society that no-one else can make. Each is a unique person, for whom relationships with other persons in community are as essential to the healthy nourishment of personhood as proper food is for the nourishment of our body. Much of the insecurity and stress felt today by people searching for their individual identity – young people especially – has its roots in the loss of community.

This *psychodiversity* is one of the most wonderful things in the world, and not only because of the constellations of acknowledgement, work and acclaim its numbers contribute, but because each is, for the ones who are graced to intuit the fire that drives this individual, beloved uniquely, and reciprocally loving. And so if we see his face in every flower, and in the form and beauty of each species a unique aspect of God, in the beauty and diversity of each self-reflective intelligence we see a different aspect on another level. And if the possibilities realised on successive levels of the organisation of matter are seen as ever-higher expressions of what God is, personhood and the inter-relating of persons is as high as we can go in framing our human acclaim.

Each of us is capable of making a contribution no other can make to the furthering of the community, which has a duty to facilitate that contribution as far as its resources permit: just as it is the duty of the individual to strive its utmost to make its unique contribution. Each individual is entitled to the same dignity, but that is not the same as saying we are all the same. Everyone is different. And it is expected that each will contribute his/her 100%, not somebody else's 100%, because each is different, but only when we are prepared to give of our talent in the service of the community are we entitled to what it has to give us. This raises the deep question of how to reconcile individual difference of effort and endeavour, of use of the talents given. This is the challenge of the parable of the Wedding Feast. And the answer is to be found in the realisation and acceptance that, like science, salvation is a community enterprise – and we should have enough on our minds to distract us from measuring the contribution our less focused brothers and sisters are making to our common enterprise. Ours not to reason why when the domain on which we toil may not have all the answers.

The song of each human life is different, as the song of each species of bird is different. We are not called upon to write books of philosophy. All we have to do is sing the song we are capable of. Some of us can only sing a few notes, maybe the same note over and over: but my melody is unique to me. And there are some among us whose song is so complex the rest of us can't follow it, though we are awed by its beauty. The library of such songs is vast; it includes the symphonies of Beethoven, Darwin's book on the pollination of orchids, Thomas Aquinas' *Summa Theologiae*, the Hubble telescope, the Large Hadron Collidor at CERN. I take great encouragement from Bernard Lonergan's admission of the many years he spent 'reaching up to the mind of Aquinas.'[33] What a lot of climbing that would mean for the rest of us! But we don't need to be discouraged by this at all; those songs are not ours to compose, though we may get to sing them too, but at the same time it is one of the measures of human capacity that nurtures in us the virtue of humility.

The pattern woven by the accumulated contributions of countless souls over millennia constitutes culture, which is an adaptation to a particular geography as much as it is the achievement of human endeavour, and endlessly varied on that account, a cultural kaleidoscope that fades gradually into monochrome under the diluting influences of material eutrophication and globalisation. Human thought is like the swirling nebulae: at any one time dispersed and apparently inchoate, going in all directions, and yet no iota is far from the next one and so in touch with the most distant, but over time seen to be patterned and directed and condensing it may be to a galaxy of stars.

Living in place

Il faut cultiver notre jardin.

Voltaire

It is in the countryside or the wilderness from which it is carved that we are most receptive to whatever nature has to teach us, in terms of biology and ecology of course most immediately, but also about the source of the harmony enfolded within, at the very heart and permeating every facet and scintilla of nature's reality. Not everybody can respond to this overwhelming revelation with an adequately articulated expression of faith, and indeed the more we try to do so the more the harmony diminishes, smothered in words, dying away finally in the abstractions of theology.

And although the disintegration discussed earlier can be attributed to a process of economic development and has been extensively analysed and explained in terms of the evolution of free market capitalism 'through the progressive dispossession of the common people of the means to feed and sustain themselves within their local communities',[34] at a deeper level it can be attributed to the decay at the heart of what is always called 'faith', which can be envisaged metaphorically perhaps as a kind of radioactive kernel emitting a life-giving warmth in a hundred thousand different ways at all the different hearths of religious expression that have developed to let it glow in and reach out from the human heart and soul.

And the place of this encounter is, in the first place, *this* place in which I grew up and find my place in the world. Later it may be enriched by rainforest and coral reef, tundra and savannah and the deep ocean, but our response to these is only an echo of a response that is born and nurtured in the place my feet walk, where the wind and birdsong are in my ears, where I can stand under trees as a child. The first rain forest lies one step beyond the threshold, in every grove of trees, in every stream. And it is not only in the jungle and the desert that this wild splendour reflects God's glory. It is on our own doorstep, if we weren't too eternally busy to stop, to look, to see, and then to wonder and praise. There is truly more to wonder at, more to bring us to our knees, than our short lifetimes can ever compass, in the pond, and along the fringe of the bog, and in the last bit of woodland in the parish.

The ideal human life is lived in a society that consists of a network of co-operative communities that is governed by an overarching religious *telos* that is guided by the best possible exercise of human reason, and whose conduct is directed by the exercise of virtue. Within the community committed to reason and virtue in this way, and especially when this community is bound to the particular land from which it draws the earth resources that support and nourish it, each of these unique persons, whatever the measure of his or her talents or limitations, has his place, has a unique role to play, and is at home. This of course is Eutopia, which many down the ages have sought and sketched the delineations of, and striven to create. But that land is to be found not somewhere else, or in some other time, neither past nor future. It is to be worked for in the present, in the place in which you are. Our task is to harmonise our human acclaim with *Das Lied von der Erde* in this place here and now. We will find much evidence of abuse and neglect due to the failure of reason and virtue. The task of restoration is a long one: but of course this is the same task of which we spoke earlier, and we must be prepared for that, and live with hope in the future as we work to heal the earth, while striving to become the best we can be ourselves within our community. But the first thing we need to do is find out where we are, and get to know our place – arriving it may be in the place from which we first began, and finding we are coming to know it for the first time.[35]

It is only when *telos* is restored as society's overarching goal that human life can be lived to the full, and at its most deeply rational. And it is only in that embrace that the individual life recovers its true dignity and harnesses its true capacity. In our own day we need to recover that beacon of reason which is also, after all, our guiding light, dimly glowing from within, in the apprehension of that 'written' revelation we always considered as independent, unmediated by and separate from rather than more deeply embedded within, that primary revelation that is creation in its fullest embrace.

Community and place

Essentially nourished though we are through encounter with creation, the individual human can only find his or her self fully through the relationships in community in which those qualities of excellence appropriate to our deep response to God – the virtues – are exercised. At an earlier stage in human evolution community might be defined in relation to the portion of the earth's surface which provided its food and shelter, and with which therefore over time it learned to develop a relationship that ensured the maintenance of its capacity to do this indefinitely: learned to live sustainably that is, essentially independent of other groups for most of its everyday requirements – raw materials, agriculture, processing skills, arts and crafts – and for the network of its sustaining relationships with others.[36]

This scale is biologically determined, a dimension of biophilia (see page 68). And just as we can only be 'at home' when we are close to the natural world, we can only be truly at home in a place with which we are *commensurate* – of such a size that we can get to know and relate to it, and feel we have taken root. My life is not lived among the stars or in the realms of the quarks, even though my mind can wander there and my life be enriched by that exploration. My life is lived in a particular place in a particular corner of the earth, on a scale that is defined by my biological nature. My ability to travel beyond the horizon merely expands my understanding of the space it defines.[37]

Once upon a time the word parochial simply meant something pertaining to one's parish. It has come over time to acquire negative connotations, to mean somebody whose outlook, interests, involvement are narrow, confined to the small area covered by the parish. But actually, the area for which we are made, meant, to spend our lives, biologically, psychologically, spiritually is the parish, not in the literal sense of an area that stops at a defining line on a map, but at the horizon where the sun rises in the morning and sets in the evening – yet a flexible horizon that expands and contracts in time and place. Body and mind and soul, we are made to live our lives anchored in this one place. Globalisation shows us all the kingdoms of the earth, which can be ours if we bow down and adore the god of materialism. The great temptation – the little variant in my life of the great temptation to which Jesus of Nazareth was subjected when, weak after 40 days of fasting in the desert he was whisked [by the devil] to a [high place] and shown all the kingdoms of the earth – is to allow ourselves to think that our human possibility is narrowed by this anchorage.

But on the contrary, as a plant can only extend its branches, reach its full stature and flower and fruit as it is meant to do, when its roots are firmly anchored and penetrate deeply into the soil of one place, our mind and spirit can extend to the most enriching limits only when similarly nourished, body and mind and spirit, by one place. It does not mean turning our back on any of the great extensions of our physical capacities that the advance of science places at our disposal. It means using them to serve that enrichment through a life informed by wisdom and virtue, *not being used by them* – which is what we have allowed to happen, to an extent so benumbing that we are scarcely aware of it any more.

Our senses and our capacities have become increasingly divorced from direct and real encounter with the earth. We have become progressively distanced from nature's touch over this last century, first by radio, then television and now in recent years by the cybernetic revolution. I still find it hard to get used to people walking through a world of birdsong inside the sound bubble of their I-Pods, with a mobile phone all but implanted in their ears, and whose substitute for community is the disembodied contact of FaceBook and UTube.

For most of human prehistory and history people's direct experience hardly extended beyond the seen horizon that was the edge of their little world. But they knew this world in the way the animal knows its niche. Their way of living was characterised by *intimacy*, an experienced closeness to the earth cut to our human measure, as it were. Such experience is *parochial*, in the original and best sense of the word. In the first place there is intimacy in our knowledge of the people who live alongside us in this home place and share our lives, developed through shared work and understanding; and secondly with the resources of this home place, knowing intimately how to use them, timber and stone and soil, to build the fabric of our cultural landscape and sustain the community it shelters. They knew every bush and every stone, every slope and shadow, the variation of its soils and what grew in them – as know it they must because upon this knowledge their very lives depended, and their future. And yet it was a winged intimacy that extended far beyond a little earth-bound land circumscribed by the horizon, reaching as it did through imagination and intellect to frame their world against the movement of the great lights of the sky and the seasons they controlled.[38]

It was among such rural societies that the series of methodologies for right living that became the earth's great religious traditions crystallised. In the case of Christianity, the New Testament is like an extended farm tour. The politicisation of the great religious traditions on the other hand is an urban development.

This is the place in which I encounter reality. It is where I come to understand what neighbour and neighbourhood means. It is where I get to experience community. It is where I encounter the other lives that lead me to contemplation of God's creation. It is what nurtures me physically (providing my food and shelter) as well as emotionally and spiritually – or it used to, before globalisation and modernity began to dissolve the sinews that bound us together and we have found ourselves drifting into our modern placelessness. This place is also the only place where my action can be real and where I can learn and practice virtue. It is easier to send money to the homeless in Calcutta than to converse with the beggar outside my gate. So we have to find our place again, or at least come to realise that we need to find it – and as we do so we find that a whole spiritual agenda, both in contemplation and practice, opens before us.

The landscape and community to which human living is adapted by nature and evolution equates broadly in terms of scale with the cadastral units that were adopted as parishes by the early church. Think of it as the cultural counterpart to the ecosystem, but much broader and richer because of the cultural embroidery we bring to overlay on it (the word parish comes from the Latin *paroecia*, which is the Greek *paroikía*, the area around my home; interestingly there is no such word in Classical Latin. It only came into use with Christianity). The sense of identity that is commensurate with the human need to belong and lead a fulfilling and purposeful life is most easily and naturally achieved on the scale of the parish, in the broader economic and ecological sense in which I have just defined it. The churches might fruitfully give thought to a development of this richer sense of what the parish could mean for human fulfillment. Nowhere perhaps can the power and potential of that sense of identity be glimpsed more clearly than in the pride, dedication and excellence attained on the field of sport in the Inter-Club GAA Championships. Team sports and warfare are essentially displacement activities, a substitute for more meaningful expressions of group identity that centre around community and food production that have been reduced, distorted or lost. Can you imagine what might be achieved if the same effort and dedication could be applied to the perfection and application of other human skills in other areas of endeavour at local level?

Ireland's parishes were mapped out at the Synod of Rathbreasail, which took place in 1111, and which oversaw the transition of the medieval Irish church from one that was based on the monasteries to one based on dioceses. The parishes were originally co-extensive with the *tuath*, the territory controlled and farmed by a clan or extended family grouping together with their servants and dependants, just as the dioceses corresponded to larger political units.[39] The parish is made up of a number of townlands of varying size, and although this is doubtless a great simplification, it is useful to imagine that these started out as individual farming units. In the course of time parish boundaries changed as the size and distribution of the population and the political situation changed, and townland boundaries even more extensively in response to more local changes in landownership, family structure, as well as political and social arrangements. The old 'civil' parishes were, however, frozen in time on the sheets of the 1st edition six-inch Ordnance Survey maps.[40]

The essence of human community

What binds community is shared purpose and meaning. In earlier stages of society that shared purpose was the production of the food that nurtures all, and each individual had a role in that common enterprise, either directly or at one remove, because the fields in which the corn grew and cattle grazed were the fields of home. Over centuries and indeed millennia, each region of the agricultural world developed a richness and diversity unique to itself, in the ways it learned to use to the fullest effect, without waste, the produce of the earth; in the arts and crafts associated with that enterprise; in the metaphors of faith that grounded it in something Beyond, something deeper, more ultimate. This cultural diversity was perhaps the greatest achievement of mankind.

The forces that have loosened and eventually broken the bonds that hold it all together, progressively and at different times and places, are easily labelled – the expansion of commerce, the development of financial systems, industrialisation, globalisation – and readily glossed with justificatory labels such as progress, growth, inevitability etc. Such developments were seldom undertaken primarily because they helped to nourish and sustain the communities at the heart of these ancient systems, but for the benefit of individuals or groups, often outside the community. In themselves all these developments can contribute to the enhancement of community, but only when applied judiciously and with foresight, and such wisdom in those empowered to make decisions and initiate action is all too often absent. Religious authority has often seen the dangers inherent in 'progress', but failed to stem the tide and indeed in any case often acted out of self interest.

The dismantling of the material framework of the essential community (i.e. one that revolves around the production of its own food) is one face of the problem and the challenge. The other is the loss of an ultimate goal. Political philosophy often provides a 'penultimate' goal, the attainment of which is often linked to a sanctioning theology (the Irish nation and the Catholic Church is the most familiar example). The achievement of independence clouds the vision of anything more 'ultimate' to be achieved, especially if it leads to greater prosperity and material well-being for a majority of people.

This is the situation we find ourselves in today. We have attained a state of material well-being that would utterly astonish a visitor from any earlier Ireland. It is, however, a prosperity only minimally anchored in the productive capacity of the land, and we have attained it at a time when the credibility of the traditional religious ethos is enormously weakened. This weakening was catalysed by the various scandals that have rocked the church in recent decades, but it has led to a radical and widespread loss of both moral and doctrinal credibility. In this lies the root of the aimlessness that increasingly characterises our society, and in particular the life of the young.

A. J. Toynbee was thinking mainly of the loss of faith in the west when he wrote in his great study of history:

> The extinction of faith is being recognised as the supreme danger to the spiritual health and even to the material existence of the Western body social – a deadlier danger by far than any of our hotly canvassed and loudly advertised political and economic maladies. To refill the spiritual vacuum is the most formidable and the most urgent of all problems that are remorselessly crowding upon the present generation.
>
> Arnold Toynbee, *Study of History*

Particular expressions of faith are moulded by cultural factors. It is difficult to disentangle the perennial elements at their core from elements conditioned by their place in history or geography, particularly from within the culture, and especially in relation to those facets shaped by religion. This perennial core is within time, incarnate, and discussion concerning it stretches human language and imagination to their limit and beyond. But their capacity is overloaded when it comes to intuition and discernment of the eternal behind the perennial. However, modern scientific man does not accept that there is in human nature a level of reaching into a higher dimension of meaning where incarnate understanding and expression are inadequate. On this account then, not everyone will be happy with a response that uses religious language, and will find it hard to see that an answer in any language other than faith is not a superior substitute, or to accept that there might be a further stage in which language slips away, and we find ourselves in a place beyond words where every being each in its own space stands, and the heart echoes in a way that leaves no room for any response other than yes.

Community and food

Human community revolves around the shared production of food. There is a profound satisfaction in producing the food that sustains me, my family and my community. The bread of life is not simply a commodity, it binds human beings with the nourishing earth, and it binds human community. It is the life blood of the web of relationships within which the human spirit is most at ease. And when this community is allowed the time and space to grow, every facet of human ingenuity and talent find expression, and there is a role for every individual in the working out of which he or she finds fulfillment, for the weak as well as the strong in mind or body. There are deep biological roots to a need that is within us to procure our own food, or to be within reach of the ones in our immediate, experienced community, who do. We are *made* to do this, and there lies the ultimate explanation for the satisfaction of gardening or traditional farming.

Now our horizons have expanded beyond the limits of the rising and setting sun, and that should be a good thing, enabling us to enrich our grasp of what human brotherhood means, to enrich our particular cultural achievement and appreciate its unique quality more proudly, mutually able to further our well-being on a material plane as well as in the sense of more deeply experiencing and appreciating the richness and further possibility of human existence.

But the expansion of horizon has been accompanied less by this deeper appreciation of what we have, this broader vision of what we may be, than by a loosening of the values embodied within local community. The loss of autonomous food production is a key factor in this loosening. It has been a progressive process, step by step that is, and there is an assumption that each stage of development therefore marks 'progress,' and it is justified by reference to this shibboleth as if it justifies everything that happens. In modern times the development that characterised any particular stage was undertaken not primarily because careful consideration showed that such development would benefit the community at large and in the long term, using sustainability and the welfare of commonwealth as yard-sticks. Of course there were elements within any particular development that could have been applied to this end, but they were applied in the interest primarily of individual or group profit – though of course this motivation is never emphasised in the promotion of development.

The most recent stage in this 'progress' (using the word now in its somewhat antiquated meaning of 'journey') sees the emergence of very large retail and commodity outlets which source their products wherever in the world these can be acquired at the lowest financial cost. This is justified as 'what the consumer wants,' but when the ramifying roots of the system are followed to their geographical origins and their social consequences explored, it is not difficult to see the corroding effects of this ultimate commodification of food and craft on the communities at both ends. J. J. Massingham was wrong to believe he was seeing the end of this process when he wrote half a century ago:

> Food comes not from the fields but from the factory; and thought is denatured as well as food. Houses are pre-fabricated and owe nothing to rock, soil or timber. Our native earth was once our home; then it became our recreation; now it is a business like any other industry, not a livelihood. Distance has become a value in itself by the obsolescence of the home-sense. The horizon rules our affairs, not the threshold and internationalism is the new word for neighbourliness.[41]

No politician is going to raise a voice in protest, however, such is the flow of the tide in this direction. No more could a reflective Seneca have stemmed the tide of the popular clamour for bread and circuses in a declining Rome. It took the advancing hordes of the uncivilised, hovering with envy and dissatisfaction on the fringes of the Empire, to do that.

The inexorable march of mechanisation, industrialisation and more recently globalisation has acted, as it were, like a form of cultural eutrophication, extinguishing the bright flame of this wonderful, kaleidoscopic legacy of rural culture. The notion of material eutrophication is one that merits closer examination. It is the diametric opposite of what is meant by the virtue of poverty, in the sense we discussed earlier on page 158. The poor in this virtuous sense are never in need – this is not destitution; it encourages us to live human life to the fullest. It was at the heart of what the great Mahatma Gandhi was about. It was also a defining element in De Valera's vision of rural Ireland, though his most famous attempt to articulate it has been the butt of sneers ever since.

> Acutely conscious though we are of the misery and desolation in which the greater part of the world is plunged, let us turn aside for a moment to that ideal Ireland that we would have. That Ireland which we dreamed of would be the home of a people who valued material wealth only as the basis of right living, of a people who were satisfied with frugal comfort and devoted their leisure to the things of the spirit – a land whose countryside would be bright with cosy homesteads, whose fields and villages would be joyous with the sounds of industry, with the romping of sturdy children, the contests of athletic youths and the laugher of comely maidens, whose firesides would be forums for the wisdom of serene old age. It would, in a word, be the home of a people living the life that God desires that man should live.[42]

It is easy to be put off by the style or the words. Yet this is what the best of those who sought national independence fought for with such passion. And it would be easy to paraphrase these words to provide an entirely similar Unionist expression of the same ideal. Indeed, it would not be difficult to translate them into language that many modern critics of developments in rural society would feel able to endorse.

Ethics and aesthetics

The landscapes in which humans feel naturally most at home are dominated by natural processes and components because of our 'innate tendency to focus on life and lifelike processes'. The main premise of the biophilia hypothesis is that human beings evolved as creatures deeply enmeshed with the intricacies of nature, and that we still have this affinity with nature ingrained in our genotype. The traditional agricultural landscape is the extension of the natural landscapes in which we are most at home.[43] The increased use we make of these landscapes must be sustainable, so that we do not compromise the opportunity for future generations. The challenge of doing this imposed constraints on the size of the population a particular locality could support. Such landscapes also resembled purely natural landscapes in that nothing was out of place, and so was an extension of the natural landscape, and in harmony with the natural human *aesthetic*.

> To the extent that each person can feel like a naturalist, the old excitement of the untrammelled world will be regained. I offer this as a formula of re-enchantment to invigorate poetry and myth: mysterious and little known organisms live within walking distance of where you sit. Splendor awaits in minute proportions.
>
> Edward O. Wilson, *Biophilia* (1984), p 139

We use the word 'aesthetic' nowadays with reference to artistic refinement – taste in furniture, art, couture etc – but it originally meant something quite different. It was used by Kant to mean the science that deals with *the conditions of sensuous perception*, and it is in something of that sense I will use it here in addressing the question of what characterises the right living space of a local community landscape, the *paroikia*.

At an earlier stage of our social development, where resources are limited and must be provided by the land under the control of the community, little or nothing was wasted – waste was something society could not afford.

With the opening up of the economy to outside influences this began to change, but gradually. Rural people in all cultures down the centuries demonstrate great ingenuity in husbanding their resources. Failure to do so could lead to disaster.[44] But once goods produced beyond the horizon enter the local economy to any extent there is radical change on several fronts. Most importantly, there is a new dependency on the outside world for these goods; if they are goods that were up to then produced *within* the community then the skills necessary to their production are now lost to it, and those employed have to find something else that gives them a sense of their work being a valued part of the *telos* of the community. Should the supply of goods be disrupted or cut off, the consequences may be serious, even disastrous, especially when the future that lies immediately ahead of us is a territory where 'we really have no idea of what it will be like, or how we will cope.'[45] We are all in this situation today, because the community of the average *paroikia* is almost entirely dependent on goods from far afield.

Secondly, the goods imported seldom come alone. They are packaged: simply at first, but with increasing sophistication as living standards rise and the 'added' in added value metamorphoses from valuable to useless. By the same token, the community is flooded with products that are neither necessary nor useful in any real sense, and are not intended to last. The environmental consequences of all this are that, increasingly as time passes, society has to deal with waste materials that are of no use to it, and in spite of provisions to deal with it centrally, much of it finds its way into an environment in which it is out of place and aesthetically wrong – not perhaps morally wrong in any familiar sense, but aesthetic does grade into ethic, because the presence of this alien waste in the environment reflects an abuse of the material resources of the earth on a multitude of levels, and/or a lessening of virtuous behaviour in the management of the earth.[46] Even on a small scale it is at variance with the landscape aesthetic that is appropriate to the good life. On the larger scale that is unfortunately all too familiar, it is an abuse of the God-endowed natural ecological balance to which our maintenance should respond, and of which our traditional ways of management are usually so careful. It is therefore a not unimportant aspect in our care for the earth, especially because so many other facets are reflected in it. Tackling it at parish level provides a focus for us to broaden our attention to environmental resource management on the broader canvas of nation and the earth itself.

Afterwords ...

For the more than 40 years since I first read of it, I have pondered with fascination the final three months of Thomas Aquinas' life. On the morning of 6 December 1273 a profound and life-altering change came over him, and he found himself unable to write. This most brilliant man, the greatest mind perhaps of all who lived in the 2nd millennium, the torrent of whose thoughts and articulation about God and creation could scarcely be bottled by the staff of emanuenses who hung on his every word, became silent. It seems most likely that he had reached a point where his body could no longer take the demands he had been placing upon it for years – an almost unbroken round of teaching, writing, preaching and praying, spending as little time as possible eating or sleeping (although the possibility of a stroke that resulted in brain damage cannot be ruled out).[1] When his personal companion Reginald of Piperno insisted upon an explanation, all Thomas could say was: 'All I have written seems like straw.' But when Reginald persisted he went further (after getting Reginald promise he would never repeat this): 'All I have written seems like straw compared to what has now been revealed to me.'

So there was something else: something that came into such searingly sharp focus as a result of his physical incapacity that his flow of words dried up. What this was, I believe, was a new realisation (making-real-for-him) of *the sheer inadequacy of words* – the truth that no conceptual framework of human concepts and sentences can express the infinite reality behind and within all that is and all that happens, not even the 40 volumes of mesmerisingly brilliant theology, philosophy and spiritual writing that had flowed from his pen. Thomas died at the age of 49 on 7 March the following year, following an accident while he was making his way to the Second Council of Lyons; he was struck by a branch of a tree leaning across the road, possibly causing a subdural haematoma from which he died some days later.

* * *

A great deal of theology resembles fleets of free-floating balloons, woven of mesmerisingly intellectual ingenuity enclosing little more than slightly warmed air, but which have lost the rope/thread that once anchored them to the reality of earthly experience – and lost touch with that heart-stopping glimpse on the conceptual horizon that fuelled the imperative to take to the air in the first place. But the real human pilgrimage is a quest on foot, step by often weary step, each planted on the earth and directed by thought that lacks wings, because we are not the angels we imagine.

The danger with god-talk (i.e. theology), with its presumption that we can discuss God as meaningfully as everyday things, is how easily we can get tangled in the web of our own words. The language we use (including mathematics and the language of science) – the only language we have – is adequate for our own experience, and it can describe it with astounding accuracy and success. But its very success can blind us to its incapacity to hold the infinity we call God, which we can only intuit through openness to our experience of the world – through immersion in the reality of the being of the world that we are graced with in our individual lives, on any one or several of many levels – through the prolonged attention of theological thinking, the more focused attention of the naturalist, but above and before all, in the encounter of everyday living …

This encounter evokes a response that evades adequate expression. We can only sing the notes our vocal chords can voice, conceive only the thoughts our minds can compute for. It is precisely because it cannot be contained in a vessel made of concept or word that such conflicting articulation is possible, from the denial of atheism through the ascetic naturalism and muted acclaim of such great theologians as John F. Post, Charley Hardwick and Henry N. Wieman, on through the mainstream dominated by the familiar great names of modern theology in their various sodalities and under their various banners, to exit the other end of faith into the bright light of everyday where all our theology blossoms in the cultural rainbow that is piety and ritual – the full-voiced polyphonic acclaim of humanity.

Art, and perhaps especially poetry, with its capacity to use words that have echoes, can better articulate the response.

Liturgy and ritual can do the same – they are not to be dismissed as if they were to be evaluated in the way laboratory design or experimental procedure must be evaluated. The profound thorough-going naturalism upon which the scientist will insist is compatible with all of the paraphernalia of religious expression, so long as we do not lose sight of the fact that they are historical, evolving, culturally-conditioned phenomena. Julian Huxley in his search for a religion without revelation or a personal God, could still find room for ritual celebration and organised worship:

> There will always remain the religious satisfaction of plunging the mind in a common social act, and always a satisfaction in a familiar ritual hallowed by time and association. There is also to many people a satisfaction in symbolism; and to others in finding, in the combined privacy and publicity of the church service, a simultaneous release from the world and from the individual self.[2]

And even for such a hard naturalist as Charley Hardwick, for whom 'God' is (no more than) Creative Event, 'the actuality in which value is grounded,'[3] piety is 'the very essence of religion'. So a naturalistic spirituality need not lead us into an emotional desert, even in the hard naturalism of such theologians as Wieman, for whom God is reduced to 'a minimum that cannot be denied', and which transposes the question of God from ontology to value.[4]

* * *

> Unless all existence is a medium of revelation, no particular revelation is possible....
>
> William Temple, *Nature, Man and God*

The idea of creation as revelation has been one of the central themes of these pages, and not merely *a* book of revelation, but *the* book. It is the actual unfolding of the cosmos and of human history that is the ultimate revelation: 'revelation is not a statement but a showing ... God speaks by deeds, not by words.'[5] 'Propositional' revelation is distilled from reflection on that unfolding, that history: 'The revelation of God is given in deeds; the doctrines of the faith are formulated by reflection on the significance of these deeds.'[6]

The diversity and beauty and complexity of living forms with which creation confronts us are, in Aquinas' god-language, the flowering of God's own self-expression, at the service of human life indeed, but existing primarily for its own sake – that is, for God's sake. The mesmerising multiplicity of species is the very etymology of creation, the ultimate word of God. Understanding, appreciating this diversity, deepens our appreciation of the language God uses. This is exegesis on a deeper, more fundamental and universal level than dissecting the language of scriptures with their layers of human fallability. This is the language that should shape the syntax of theology. Such a theology would break the mould in which we have confined the infinite God with the fairy tales of the god-talk of our childhood, keeping him or her to a size we are comfortable with. But God's comfort may not be ours, shaped as our comfort is by the physical which is dominant in our being.[7]

* * *

> Man cannot afford to be a naturalist, to look at Nature directly, but only with the side of his eye. He must look through and beyond her.
>
> Henry David Thoreau, *Journals*

I have tried to convey something of the feeling bordering on ecstasy with which anyone who has embarked upon serious involvement in the study and proper encounter with any group of plants or animals is imbued – with limited success perhaps, because it is very difficult to find words that can contain it. It matters little what group is adopted for study. It can be sea anemones or frogs, fungi or mosses, barnacles or fungi; it can be bacteria, but for the greatest number it is the most immediately accessible flowers or birds (remember Linnaeus' chambers, back on page 65). The sense of amazement and awe, of wonder and admiration is overwhelming, and a sense that Purpose with a capital P that can embrace all contingency and chance is at the heart of things. Vladimir Nabokov described his feeling when he was among his beloved butterflies and the plants that nourished them as 'ecstasy, and behind the ecstasy something else, which is hard to explain. It is like a momentary vacuum into which rushes all that I love. A sense of oneness with sun and stone. A thrill of gratitude to whom it may concern – to the contrapuntal genius of human fate or to tender ghosts humouring a lucky mortal.'[8]

Without the disciplined experience of this close encounter it is impossible to appreciate the psycho-spiritual impact of such study of the diversity of living things, although we brush against it every time we walk through the natural world, touching the threads that adorn the hem of infinity. Jan Swammerdam was one of the first to have the benefit of the microscope for such close encounter: 'Those who would avoid being imposed upon, should study nature in herself; for many fallacies and errors have crept into the writings of preceding ages, that people cannot but be led astray by them, as often taking things upon trust, they neglect to see for themselves.'[9]

Those who have not had the privilege of such encounter with life's incomprehensible diversity should be slow to pontificate on the meaning of the universe. For this is what the stars, in their forward quest in time, are about. And how are we, dippers on the narrow stream of intellect, to know the wonder of a world that lies beyond its familiar and thrilling narrows?

Syngefield
12th May 2009

Notes

CHAPTER ONE

1. An excellent account of the history and progress of science will be found in John Gribbin's *Science, A History 1543-2001* (Penguin Books, 2003).

2. The 'proper' name for the rod of a sundial: Eratosthenes' stick in other words!

3. Aristotle, *De Anima* III, 7.

4. The story of Alexandria is beautifully summarised in Carl Sagan's *Cosmos* (Ballintyne Books, 1985), pp 12-21 and 333-337, 370-415; see also Michael Deakin, *Hypatia of Alexandria: Mathematician and Martyr* (Prometheus Books, 2007).

5. *Aquinas. Selected Philosophical Writings*, selected by Timothy McDermott (Oxford University Press, 1993).

6. Brian Clegg, *The First Scientist: A Life of Roger Bacon* (Constable and Robinson, 2003); James Blish, *Doctor Mirabilis* (Arrow, 1976).

7. See Stillman Drake, *Galileo at Work: His Scientific Biography* (Dover Publications, 1995).

8. Brian Greene, *The Elegant Universe: Superstrings, Hidden Dimensions, and the Quest for the Ultimate Theory* (Vintage, 2000), pp. 94-97. For a more detailed account see http://en.wikipedia.org/wiki/Double-slit_experiment

9. In fact, although he argued this strongly, Descartes kept the possibility that animals had feelings similar to ours open: 'I do not think it is thereby proved that there is not, since the human mind does not reach into their hearts' (René Descartes, 'Animals are Machines', in *Environmental Ethics: Divergence and Convergence*, eds S. J. Armstrong and R. G. Botzler (New York, McGraw-Hill 1993), pp 281-285.

10. Alexander Hellmans and Bryan Bunch, *The History of Science and Technology: A Browser's Guide to the Great Discoveries, Inventions, and the People Who Made Them from the Dawn of Time to Today* (Houghton Mifflin Harcourt, 2004).

11. Dava Sobel, *Longitude: The True Story of a Lone Genius Who Solved the Greatest Scientific Problem of His Time* (Penguin, 1996).

12. Aristotle, Book 1 of *On the Heavens and the World*.

13. Newton wrote in a letter to Robert Hooke 'If I have seen further it is by standing on the shoulders of giants.' (The famous quotation was in fact used by many others before Newton).

14. Martin Heidegger, 'Holderlin and the Essence of Poetry,' in *Existence and Being*, Intro, Brock, Werner (South Bend, Ind, Regnery/Gateway, 1979), page 277.

15. Albert Einstein, 'Physics and reality' (1936), reprinted in A. Einstein, *Out of My Later Years* (Philosophical Library, New York, 1950), p 59.

16. Vaclav Smil, *Enriching the Earth. Fritz Haber, Carl Bosch, and the Transformation of World Food Production* (MIT Press, 2001), especially pp 226-231.

17. Wendell Berry, 'Solving for pattern.' Chapter 9 in *The Gift of Good Land. Further Essays Cultural and Agricultural* (New York, North Point Press, 1981).

18. Richard Powers, *The Gold Bug Variations* (Harper Perennial, 1992), p 411.

19. Hans Küng, *The Beginning of All Things. Science and Religion* (Eerdmans, 2007), p 37 (my italics).

20. Martin Rees, *Our Final Century? Will the Human Race Survive the Twenty-First Century?* (London, 2004).

CHAPTER TWO

1. http://hubblesite.org/gallery; see also: http://www.wordwizz.com/pwrsof10.htm

2. Brian Swimme and Thomas Berry, *The Universe Story From the Primordial Flaring Forth to the Ecozoic Era, A Celebration of the Unfolding of the Cosmos* (HarperCollins 1992, reprint edition 1994); Hoimar von Ditfurth, *Children of the Universe. The Tale of Our Existence* (George, Allen and Unwin, 1975); Nellie McLaughlin, *Out of Wonder. The Evolving Story of the Universe* (Veritas, 2004). See also: http://en.wikipedia.org/wiki/The_Great_Story

3. John Gribbin, op. cit.

4. Paul Davies, *The Fifth Miracle. The Search for the Origin of Life* (Allen Lane, The Penguin Press, 1998). 'The obvious conclusion, enshrined as the Cosmogenetic Principle, is that in this universe there are entirely natural powers of form production that, when given the proper conditions, will create galaxies; each successive level of differentiation has its own interactions, qualitatively and quantitatively different from other levels. Each is a distinct "world".'

5. *The Universe Story*, p 54.

6. *The Universe Story*, p 34.

7. *The Universe Story*, pp 34-35.

8. *The Universe Story*, p 63.

9. *The Universe Story*, p 64.

CHAPTER THREE

1. For a fascinating account see Marcus Chown, *The Magic Furnace. The Search for the Origins of Atoms* (Oxford University Press, 2001).

2. That's the matter we can see. But in fact most of the universe is invisible. As well as the bright stars and galaxies we can see with the aid of telescopes, there is at least ten times as much 'dark matter' about which we know next to nothing.

3. Piers Bizony, *Atom* (Icon Books, 2007).

4. There is a wonderful account in John Gribbin's *Companion to the Cosmos* (Little Brown, 1996).

5. George Musser, *The Complete Iditot's Guide to String Theory* (Alpha Books, 2008).

6. For further detail see Roger Penrose, *The Road to Reality: a complete guide to the laws of the universe* (Alfred A. Knopf / Jonathan Cape, 2004).

7. If the density of matter in the universe is more than 11 atoms of hydrogen per cm^3, the universe will expand forever; if it is less than this it will contract.

8. For more: John Gribbin, *The Universe, A Biography* (Allen Lane, 2007); *Q is for Quantum. Particle Physics from A to Z* (Weidenfeld and Nicholson, 2002); *Get a Grip on Physics* (Barnes and Noble, 2003).

9. Robert M. Hazen, Dominic Papineau, Wouter Bleeker, Robert T. Downs, John M. Ferry, Timohy J. McCoy, Dimitri A. Sverjensky and Hexiong Yang (2008). Mineral evolution, *American Mineralogist* 93 (11-12) (2008), 1693-1720.

10. G. F. H. Smith, *Gemstones* (Methuen, 1958; 13th edition revised by F. C. Phillips); J. F. Kirkaldy, *Minerals and Rocks in Colour* (Blandford Press, 1968, 2nd edition).

CHAPTER FOUR

1. D. Dixon, I. Jenkins, R. Moody and A. Zhuralev, *Cassell's Atas of Evolution* (Cassell & Co, 2001); Steven M. Stanley, *Earth System History* (Freeman, 2005; 2nd edition); Stephen Jay Gould, *The Book of Life* (Ebury Hutchinson, 1993).

2. Tectonics is the study of the mechanisms and results of large-scale movement of the earth's crust.

3. Peter J. Wylie, *The Way The Earth Works. An Introduction To The New Global Geology And Its Revolutionary Development* (John Wiley and Sons, 1973).

4. Andrew Sleeman, Brian McConnell and Sarah Gately, *Understanding Earth Processes, Rocks and the Geological History of Ireland* (Geological Survey of Ireland, 2004).

5. Ted Nield, *Supercontinent. Ten Billion Years in the Life of Our Planet* (Harvard University Press, 2007).

CHAPTER FIVE

1. An understanding of chemistry and biology enhances your ability to appreciate the sheer mind-boggling wonder of what cosmogenesis and the evolution of life are about enormously. Readers without a ground-

ing in these sciences who can find the time should consider working their way through a good introductory textbook in each of these disciplines. The number of wonderful books that could be recommended for this task is enormous. In chemistry an excellent basic text is Frederick A. Bettelheim, William H. Brown, Mary K. Campbell and Shawn O. Farrell, *Introduction to Organic and Biochemistry* (Brooks Cole, 2008, 7th edition). Among the best introductory texts in biology is Neil A. Campbell and Jane B. Reece, *Biology* (Benjamin Cummings, 2004, 7th edition).

2. Something that defies the laws of nature and is brought about by a supernatural agency.

3. Utterly unexpected, extraordinary and marvellous.

4. Davies, *The Fifth Miracle*, p 203.

5. Darwin's great *Origin of Species* is still a wonderful book to read; for an abbreviated version see *The Illustrated Origin of Species by Charles Darwin. Abridged and Introduced by Richard E. Leakey* (Faber and Faber, 1979). For a good up-to-the-minute introduction see Jerry Coyne, *Why Evolution is True* (Oxford University Press, 2008).

6. A. H. Sturtevant and Edward B. Lewis, *A History of Genetics* (Cold Spring Harbor Laboratory Press, 2001); see also L. C. Dunn, *A Short History of Genetics: The Development of the Main Lines of Thought, 1864-1939* (Iowa State Press, History of Science and Technology Reprint Series, 1991).

7. Paul Davies, op. cit.

8. Notice that there are different 'realms' of existence; we (and everything else on earth) are in the middle, God and his angels are up in the heavens somewhere, and the damned in hell are down in the foundations.

9. *The Works of William Paley D.D.* (Edinburgh, Peter Brown and Thomas Nelson, 1830); *Natural Theology*, pp. 435-554.

10. J. Howard Moore, *The Universal Kinship* (1905; Centaur Press, Kinship Library Reprint 1992), p 319.

11. The phrase originated with Charles Kingsley, *The Water-babies* (1886), p 307.

12. Genesis 1:26.

13. Quoted in James Reston, *Galileo, A Life* (HarperCollins, NY, 1994), p 461.

14. Theodosius Dobzhansky (1973), 'Nothing in Biology Makes Sense Except in the Light of Evolution', *The American Biology Teacher* 35 (1973), 125-129.

15. Sir Thomas Browne, *Religio Medici*.

16. John Paul II: 'Cosmology and Fundamental Physics' *Address to the Pontifical Academy of Science*, 3 October 1981.

17. Mary Midgley, *Evolution as a Religion* (Routledge, 2002, 2nd edition).

18. *John Paul on Science and Religion: Reflections on the New View from Rome*, eds Robert J. Russell, William R. Stoeger and George V. Coyne

(Vatican Observatory / University of Notre Dame Press, 1990).

19. *Entia non sunt multiplicanda sine necessitate*: if something can be explained without assuming this or that hypothetical entity, then such entities should be excluded; in other words, we should always choose the explanation that requires the fewest possible number of causes: a potentially cut-throat instrument we all, admittedly, seem to unsheath only when it suits us, and apply selectively: and of course never on ourselves, cf Bertrand Russell, *History of Western Philosophy* (Allen and Unwin, 2002) pp 462-463.

20. Eric J. Chaisson, *Epic of Evolution: Seven ages of the cosmos* (Columbia University Press, 2006).

21. D'Arcy Wentworth Thompson, *Aristotle as Biologist* (Oxford University Press, 1913.

22. Albert the Great, *Man and the beasts: De animalibus* (books 22-26), trs James Scanlan (Binghamton, NY, 1987).

23. Edward O. Wilson and Frances M. Peter (eds.), *Biodiversity* (Washington, National Academy Press, 1988).

24. Anna Pavord, *The Naming of Names. The Search for Order in the World of Plants* (Bloomsbury, 2005).

25. Colin Tudge, *The Variety of Life: A Survey and a Celebration of All the Creatures that Have Ever Lived* (Oxford University Press, 2000); Lynn Margulis and Karlene V. Schwartz, *Five Kingdoms. An Illustrated Guide to the Phyla of Life on Earth* (New York, Freeman and Company, 1998, 3rd edition); R. S. K. Barnes ed, *The Diversity of Living Organisms* (Blackwell Science, 1988).

26. John L. Howland, *The Surprising Archaea: Discovering Another Domain of Life* (Oxford University Press, 2000).

27. See *The Universe Story*, chapter 7.

28. Dan L. Perlman and Glenn Adelson, *Biodiversity* (Blackwell Science, 1997).

29. Linnaeus, *Amoenitates Academicae* Ed 2, Vol VII, 387–388.

30. John Feehan, *County Offaly: The State of the Wild 2007*, Offaly County Council, p 13.

31. Bob Holmes, 'Life unlimited,' *New Scientist* 2016: 10 February 2006.

32. See *The Universe Story*, chapter 6.

33. Garry Hamilton, 'The unsung heroes of evolution,' *New Scientist* 2671: 27 August 2008.

34. Where HGT is effected mainly by the action of viruses. Indeed, some geneticists believe that as much as 40-50 per cent of human DNA has originated in this way, sometimes across great taxonomic distances, and that it is not all 'junk' DNA. Some of it performs vital functions; for instance, the human gene known as 'syncytin,' which is essential for placenta formation, is of viral origin. See *New Scientist* 27 August 2008, p 38.

35. Rudolph S. De Groot, *Functions of nature: Evaluation of nature in environmental planning, management and decision making* (Amsterdam, Wolters-

Noordhoff, 1992); Stephen R. Kellert, *The Value of Life: Biological Diversity And Human Society* (Island Press, 1995); Stephen R. Kellert, *Kinship to Mastery: Biophilia in Human Evolution and Development* (Island Press, 1997).

36. J. H. Heerwagen and G. H. Orians, 'Humans, Habitats, and Aesthetics' in S. R. Kellert and E. O. Wilson eds, *The Biophilia Hypothesis* (Island Press, 1993), pp 138-72.

37. E. O. Wilson, *Biophilia: the Human Bond with Other Species* (Harvard University Press, 1984); S. R. Kellert and E. O. Wilson, *The Biophilia Hypothesis*.

38. John Feehan, 'Millennial thoughts on the changing landscape,' Inaugural World Landscape Lecture, in R. O'Regan ed, *Third Irish Landscape Forum: Through the Eye of the Artist* (1988), pp 74-81.

39. William Hudson, *Idle Days in Patagonia* (1893); see p 218.

40. Traherne, *Centuries of Meditations: The First Century*, 13.

41. Henry David Thoreau in his essay 'Walking' (*Nature Writing: the Tradition in English*, eds Robert Finch, John Elder, p 192).

42. Traherne, *Centuries of Meditations: The First Century*, 2.

43. Sean McDonagh, *The Death of Life. The Horror of Extinction* (The Columba Press, 2004).

44. For an overview of the magnitude of the crisis, scroll slowly through the titles of the links listed under http://www.well.com/~davidu/extinction.html

45. Dan L. Perlman and Glenn Adelson, *Biodiversity. Exploring Values and Priorities in Conservation* (Blackwell Science, 1997), p 90.

46. Richard Leakey and Roger Lewin, *The Sixth Extinction* (Weidenfeld and Nicolson, 1995).

47. Perlman and Adelson, op. cit., p 91.

48. This is the last line of Darwin's *Origin of Species*.

49. Stephen Jay Gould, *Wonderful Life: The Burgess Shale and the Nature of History* (Norton, 1990).

50. St Augustine, *The City of God*, xii, 4.

51. St Augustine, *The City of God*, xi, 22.

52. '... *distinctio rerum et multitudo est ex intentione primi agentis, quod est Deus. Produxit enim res in esse propter suam bonitatem communicandam creaturas, et per eas repraesentandam. Et quia per unam creaturam sufficienter repraesentari non potest, produxit multas creaturas et diversas, ut quod deest uni ad repraesentandam divinam bonitatem, suppleatur ex alia: nam bonitas quae in Deo est simpliciter et uniformiter, in creatures est multipliciter et divisim.'* Thomas Aquinas, *Summa Theologiae* 1a47.1.

53. Leonard J. Bowman, 'The Cosmic Exemplarism of Bonaventure,' *The Journal of Religion* 55 (2), (April 1975), pp 181-198, (University of Chicago Press).

54. In other words, earlier stages in the Self-realisation that attains the possibility of conscious realisation in humanity and actual realisation (albeit historically and culturally conditioned) in the mind and life of

Jesus of Nazareth; c.f. John Macquarrie, *Jesus Christ in Modern Thought* (SCM Press, 1990).

55. Richard Dawkins, *The Ancestor's Tale: A Pilgrimage to the Dawn of Evolution* (Mariner Books, 2005).

56. *Creavit in coelo Angelos, in terra vermiculos; non superior in illis, non inferior in istis. Sicut enim nulla manus Angelum, ita nulla posset creare vermiculum,* Augustine, *Liber soliloquiorum animae ad deum.*

57. John Feehan, 'The Fading Rainbow,' *Resurgence* 203, 12-14.

58. Isak Dinesen (Karen Blixen), *Out of Africa* (Putnam, 1937).

59. G. K. Chesterton, *St Thomas Aquinas* (London, Hodder and Stoughton, 1933), p 210.

60. John Feehan, 'The Depths of Revelation in Creation,' *Doctrine and Life* 49(2), 68-77.

61. John Muir, *The Mountains of California* (1894), which contains a wonderfully lyrical account of the American dipper (*Cinclus mexicanus*). Our species is *Cinclus cinclus*.

62. 1605-82; *Religio Medici* (the religion of a doctor) was first published in 1642.

63. John Muir, *A Thousand-Mile Walk to the Gulf,* chapter 6 (1916; reprinted Mariner Books, 1998).

64. http://en.wikipedia.org/wiki/March_of_the_Penguins

65. William Hudson, *Idle Days in Patagonia* (1893).

66. Colin Tudge, 'Religion can survive if it embraces the true spirit of science,' *New Statesman*, 21 January 2002. (The New Statesman Essay – Set thine house in order).

67. J. Howard Moore, *The Universal Kinship* (1905; Library Reprint, Centaur Press 1992).

68. Aldo Leopold, *A Sand County Almanac, and Sketches Here and There* 1948, (Oxford University Press, New York, 1987), pp 129-132.

69. John Muir, *The Story of My Boyhood and Youth* (1913); reprinted in *The Wilderness Journeys*, Canongate Classics 67 (1996), p 41.

70. J. Howard Moore, *The Ethical Kinship* (concluding section of *The Universal Kinship*), p 328

71. Muir, *A Thousand-Mile Walk to the Gulf,* p 10.

72. Roy Campbell, *Selected Poems* (London, The Saint Austin Press, 2003).

73. Thomas Huxley, *Evolution and Ethics* (1894), Note 12.

74. Douglas Chadwick, *The Grandest of Lives: Eye to Eye with Whales* (Sierra Club Books, 2006); Philip Hoare, *Leviathan or, The Whale* (London, Fourth Estate, 2008).

75. Job 41:33-34.

76. John Feehan (2005), 'Community Development: the Spiritual Dimension,' *Perspectives on Community Development in Ireland* 1(1), 63-74 (2005); 'Creation as Revelation: A New Ethic Towards the Living World,' in J. Scally ed, *A Just Society? Ethics and Values in Contemporary Ireland* (Dublin, The Liffey Press, 2003), pp 93-102.

77. Lynne U. Sneddon, Victoria A. Braithwaite and Michael J. Gentle, 'Do fishes have nociceptors? Evidence for the evolution of a vertebrate sensory system,' *Proc. R. Soc. Lond.* B (2003) 270, 1115–1121.

78. John Feehan, *By the Grace of God*, XIV.

79. Douglas Botting, *Humboldt and the Cosmos* (Sphere Books, 1973).

80. John Feehan, 'The fading rainbow,' *Resurgence* 203 (November/December 2000), pp 12-14.

81. Rachel Carson, 'Help your child to wonder,' *Woman's Home Companion*, July 1956; download at http://training.fws.gov/history/carson/carsonwonder.pdf

82. Ibid.

83. Paul Davies, *The Fifth Miracle*, pp 129-150.

84. James Lovelock, *Gaia: a New Look at Life on Earth* (Oxford University Press, 1979; new edition, 2000).

85. Jonathan Porritt, *Playing Safe: Science and the Environment* (Thames and Hudson, 2002), p 122.

86. Fred Pearce, 'Gaia, Gaia, don't go away,' *New Scientist* 28 May 1994.

87. James Lovelock, *The Practical Science of Planetary Medicine* (London, Gaia Books, 1991).

88. James Lovelock, *The Ages of Gaia: A Biography of Our Living Earth* (Oxford University Press, 1988; new edition 1996).

89. The section on emergent probability has already appeared in a substantially similar form in 'Beyond Omega,' *Studies* 96 (383) (2007), pp 283-294.

90. The best account of emergent probability and its significance is found in Bernard Lonergan's *Insight* (1957), but the concept is central to the thinking of many theologians, especially Arthur Peacocke.

91. Eric J. Chaisson, *Epic of Evolution: Seven Ages of Cosmos*; Hoimar von Ditfurth, *The Origins of Life. Evolution as Creation* (Harper and Row, 1982).

92. Consciously or otherwise the germ of the concept of inherent potentiality is to be found in the work of Henri Bergson, specifically in his concepts of 'elan vital' and his 'tendency theory'.

93. Paul Davies, *The Fifth Miracle,* p 203; see also Paul Davies, *The Cosmic Blueprint* (Penguin, 1987).

94. Michael Shermer, *Scientific American*, January 2003.

95. Plato, *Phaedrus* 278a.

96. These are the concluding words of Darwin's *The Origin of the Species* (6th edition, 1892).

97. James Jeans, *The Mysterious Universe* (Macmillan, 1930).

98. Henri Bortoft, *The Wholeness of Nature. Goethe's Way of Science* (Floris Press, 1996); David Abram, *The Spell of the Sensuous. Perception and Language in a More-Than-Human World* (Vintage Books, 1997).

99. 'On a Piece of Chalk' was first delivered in 1865 as a lecture 'to the working men of Norwich'; published in Macmillan's *Magazine* in 1868

and in Volume VII, *Discourses: Biological & Geological*, of Thomas Huxley's *Collected Essays*.
100. Quoted in Ladislaus Boros, *Hope*, pp 113-114.

CHAPTER SIX

1. This is known as the competitive exclusion principle.
2. Roger Penrose, *New Scientist 50th Anniversary Special*, 18 November 2006, p 34.
3. Paul Davies, *The Mind of God*.
4. Mary Evelyn Tucker ed, *Evening Thoughts. Reflecting on Earth as Sacred Community. Thomas Berry* (San Francisco, Sierra Club Books, 2006).
5. 'Faith, Reason and the University,' Lecture of Benedict XVI at the University of Regensburg, 12 September 2006.
6. Address by Patriarch Bartholomew at the environmental symposium held at Santa Barbara, California, 8 November 1997; quoted in Roger S. Gottlieb ed, *This Sacred Earth: Religion, Nature, Environment* (Routledge, 2004, 2nd edition).
7. Alister McGrath, *The Re-enchantment of Nature. Science, Religion and the Human Sense of Wonder* (Hodder and Stoughton, 2002).

CHAPTER SEVEN

1. David Abram, *The Spell of the Sensuous. Perception and Language in a More-Than-Human World* (Vintage, 1996).
2. Stephan Harding, *Animate Earth. Science, Intuition and Gaia* (Green Books, 2006).
3. Karl Popper (*The Logic of Scientific Discovery*, London 1934; first English edition 1959) demonstrated that intuition is a key element in discovery, and also that no scientific theory can be a complete ('positivist') account of the phenomenon it investigates; see also Michael Polanyi, *Personal Knowledge. Towards a Post Critical Philosophy* (London, Routledge, 1958; 2nd edition 1998).
4. Lord Byron, *Childe Harold's pilgrimage, Canto the Fourth*, CLXXVIII.
5. John Muir, *My First Summer in the Sierra* (Boston, Houghton Mifflin, 1911; Sierra Club Books edition 1988), p 110.
6. 'To have an insight into primary [that is archaic] religion, and perhaps into any living religion, is to have some grasp of how one can have a form of awareness which is preconceptual, mediated largely through feeling and essentially imbued with value.' Keith Ward, *Religion and Revelation* (Oxford University Press, 1994), p 71; see also Keith Ward, *Images of Eternity* (Darton, Longman and Todd, 1987).
7. Note in passing the etymology of the word: *tremens* means 'that which makes to tremble:' it can be terrifying (and in a sense negative), or it can arouse a worshipful (in a sense positive) response.
8. Alister McGrath, op cit., pp 150-151.
9. Y. Ohtsuka, N. Yabunaka and S. Takayama, 'Shinrin-yoku (forest-air

bathing and walking) effectively decreases blood glucose levels in diabetic patients,' *International Journal of Biometeorology* (Feb 1998) 41(3), 125-7; see also http://www.terrain.org/articles/14/maloof.htm

10. James Randerson, 'Wasps sniff out danger,' *New Scientist* 10 August 2002, p 20.

11. As early as 1794 Lazaro Spalanzani made this claim, but the idea was scoffed at until in 1940 Donald Griffin confirmed this and called the phenomenon 'echolocation'.

12. An intimation is not a hunch or vague notion: it means penetrating to the heart of something (the word derives from the Latin *intimus*, inmost).

13. 1 Kings 19:11-13.

14. W. H. Hudson, *Idle Days in Patagonia* (1893).

15. Colin Tudge, *Resurgence* 216 (January-February 2003).

16. The criticism of science made here is that it fails to acknowledge a greater depth to reality and the experience of reality than can be observed and measured. It does not say that science should extend its remit to include this deeper level, because in any case it exceeds our ability to assess it in dimensional terms and so will remain immeasurable. It is therefore evasive in this sense, and the reality of such experience may be denied by someone whose encounter with the creation has been insufficiently contemplative. There are theologians who would argue further that science is insufficiently rational in another sense: in the sense that our understanding of the laws of nature is incomplete, but as it becomes progressively less so occurrences and phenomena such as miracles, ESP or providential events may be explicable within a naturalistic framework and not require the intervention of an outside God. This view is given theological expression in the work of John Polkingthorne, Arthur Peacocke and Christopher Knight (among others): 'It is quite possible to see "the laws of nature" that are perceptible to the scientist as representing no more than a "low level" manifestation of what St Maximos calls the characteristic "logoi" of created things', (Christopher C. Knight, 'Emergence, Naturalism and Panentheism: An Eastern Christian Perspective.' Response to Arthur Peacocke's essay in *All that is. A Naturalistic Faith for the Twenty-First Century* (ed.Philip Clayton; Minneapolis, Fortress Press, 2007), pp 81-92.

CHAPTER EIGHT

1. Philip McShane, *Plants and Pianos: Two Essays in Advanced Methodology* (Dublin, Milltown Institute, 1971).

2. Konrad Lorenz, *King Solomon's Ring: New Light on Animals' Ways* (1949; new edition: Plume, 1997)

3. Michael Novak, *No-one sees God: The Dark Night of Atheists and Believers* (Doubleday, 2008).

4. Augustine, *De Doctrina Christiana* 1.6.6; see James K. A. Smith,

'Between prediction and silence: Augustine on how (not) to speak of God.' *Heythrop Journal* XLI (2000), pp 66–86.

5. See, for example, Charley D. Hardwick, *Events of Grace: Naturalism, Existentialism, and Theology* (Cambridge University Press, 1996).

6. Martin Buber, quoted in Hans Küng, *The Beginning of All Things*, pp 103-104.

7. Christopher Hitchens, *god is not Great. How Religion Poisons Everything* (New York, Twelve Books, 2007).

8. Genesis 11: 4, 6.

9. Alister Hardy, *Darwin and the Spirit of Man* (Collins, 1982).

10. There is a vast literature on this! Among the most forceful exposés is Daniel Dennett, *Darwin's Dangerous Idea: Evolution and the Meanings of Life* (Simon and Schuster, 1996).

11. Anthony Flew and Roy Abraham Varghese, *There Is a God: How the World's Most Notorious Atheist Changed His Mind,* HarperOne (2009).

12. For example, McGrath, op. cit., Novak, op. cit.

13. Mary Midgley, *Evolution as a Religion* (1985).

14. Julian Huxley, *Religion Without Revelation* (Original edition 1927; *The New Thinker's Library*, Greenwood Press Reprint, new edition, 1979).

15. Huxley, op. cit.

16. For an elaboration of the notion of the emergence or realisation of the fullness of human possibility in the life of Jesus see the work of Arthur Peacocke: *All that is. A Naturalistic Faith for the Twenty-First Century* (ed Philip Clayton; Minneapolis, Fortress Press, 2007); *Paths from Science Towards God: The End of all Our Exploring* (Oxford, One World, 2001); *Evolution. The Disguised Friend of Faith? Selected Essays* (Templeton Foundation Press, 2004).

17. Thomas Jefferson, *The Life and Morals of Jesus of Nazareth* (1820).

18. The philosophy of René Girard takes a profoundly insightful (and equally provocative) perspective on this; see *Violence and the Sacred* (Baltimore, Johns Hopkins University Press, 1977); for an introduction to the thought of René Girard see James G. Williams ed, *The Girard Reader* (New York, Crossroad, 1996).

19. Anthony Flew, op. cit.

20. Julian Huxley, op. cit.

21. Eye hath not seen, nor ear heard, neither have entered into the heart of man, the things which God hath prepared for them that love him (1 Corinthians 2:9).

22. Hans Küng, *Beginning*, p 205; see also Hans Küng and Walter Jens (with contributions by Dietrich Niethammer and Albin Eser), *A Dignified Dying. A Plea for Personal Responsibility* (London, SCM Press, 1995).

23. A. R. Peacocke, *Paths from Science Towards God: The End of all Our Exploring* (Oxford, One World, 2001), pp 47-48.

24. Quoted at the very end of Rachel Carson's *A Sense of Wonder*.

25. John Feehan, 'Beyond Omega,' *Studies* 96 (383) (2007), pp 283-294.

26. Ed Samuel J. Looker (London, Lutterworth Press, 1948).

27. Pierre Teilhard de Chardin, *The Phenomenon of Man* (Collins and Harper and Row, 1959).

28. *Mind* 70 (1961), 99-106; reprinted in Medawar's book *Pluto's Republic* (Oxford University Press, 1984).

29. Jacques Monod, *Chance and Necessity* (Knopf, 1971).

30. John F. Haught, *Is Nature Enough? Meaning and Truth in the Age of Science* (Cambridge University Press, 2006).

31. Arthur Peacocke, *Paths from Science Towards God*, p 9.

32. H.G. Wells, 'The Discovery of the Future,' *Nature* 65 (1902), pp 326-331.

CHAPTER NINE

1. William M. Miller, Jr, *A Canticle for Leibowitz* (1960; Orbit Reprint 1993), p 303.

2. Arthur Peacocke, *Paths from Science Towards God*, p 147.

3. Albert Einstein, 'Science and Religion,' *Nature* 146 (1940), page 605.

4. Thomas Traherne, *Centuries of Meditations; First Century*, 18, 28. (P. J. & A. E. Dobell, 1950).

5. Preface to Hugh O'Donnell's *Eucharist and the Living Earth* (The Columba Press, 2007).

6. David R. Montgomery, *Dirt. The Erosion of Civilization* (University of California Press, 2007).

7. Fred Pearce, *When the Rivers run dry. What happens when our water runs out?* (Eden Project Books, 2006).

8. Fred Pearce, *The Last Generation. How Nature Will Take Her Revenge for Climate Change* (Eden Project Books, 2006).

9. Genesis 2.19.

10. Traherne, *Meditations, First Century*, 14.

11. Hugh O'Donnell, *Eucharist and the Living Earth*.

12. The 'garment of righteousness' of Isaiah 61:10: 'I will rejoice greatly in the Lord; My soul will exult in my God, for He has clothed me with garments of salvation; He has wrapped me with a robe of righteousness, as a bridegroom decks himself with a garland and as a bride adorns herself with her jewels.'

13. *Canon Law: Ecclesiastical Ministry* (1771).

14. Hans Küng, *The Beginning of All Things*, p 82.

15. Henri Poincaré, *Science and Hypothesis* (1902; Dover Reprint 1951).

16. *Life and Letters of T. H. Huxley* Vol 1 (New York, Appleton, 1913).

17. Francois de Salignac de La Mothe, *Fenelon, The Seeking Heart* (Library of Spiritual Classics, Seedsowers reprint, 1992).

18. Ladislaus Boros, *Living in Hope. Future Perspectives in Christian Thought* (New York, Herder and Herder, 1971), p 43.

19. 1 Corinthians 2:10.

20. 1 Corinthians 13 (*Revised Standard Version*, 1989).

21. Matthew 22:37-40.

22. Matthew 10:16.

23. Matthew 25:1-13.

24. George Sheehan, *Going the Distance: one man's journey to the end of his life* (Random House/Villard, 1996).

25. Summa I-II, q.lxi, aa2 and 4; see *Catholic Encyclopedia* under 'virtue.'

26. Matthew 18:22

27. Leland J. White, 'Romans 1:26-27: The Claim that Homosexuality is Unnatural,' in Patricia Beattie Jung with Joseph Andrew Coray eds, *Sexual Diversity and Catholicism* (Collegeville, MN, The Liturgical Press, 2001), p 134.

28. 'What is said about God on the basis of faith must be related to what is felt and experienced by man in the ordinary stuff of his life – and that means a theological method far wider than that provided by the older Word of God or the newer hermeneutical theologies of the continent of Europe.' Gabriel Moran, *The New Community. Religious Life in an Era of Change* (Herder and Herder, 1970), p 25: commenting on Langdon Gilkey, *Naming the Whirlwind: the Renewal of God-Language* (New York, 1969), p 201.

29. Philosophically-informed readers will note that this brings us to the threshold of the domain over which Alasdair MacIntyre rules. They will also probably agree its language makes much of his thought very difficult of access for the non-philosopher. See *After Virtue: A Study in Moral Theory* (University of Notre Dame Press; 2nd edition, 1984).

30. Jared Diamond, *Collapse: How Societies Choose to Fail or Succeed* (Viking Adult, 2004).

31. 'Faith, Reason and the University,' Lecture of Benedict XVI at the University of Regensburg, 12 September 2006.

32. Hans Küng, *The Beginning of All Things. Science and Religion* (Eerdmans, 2007), p 53.

33. Bernard Lonergan, *Insight. A Study of Human Understanding* (Longmans, 1957; Students' revised edition of 1958), p 748.

34. Frances Hutchinson, *What Everybody Really Wants to Know About Money* (Jon Carpenter Publishing, 1998); Richard Douthwaite, *The Growth Illusion: How Economic Growth Has Enriched the Few, Impoverished the Many and Endangered the Planet* (The Lilliput Press, 1992; revised edition 1999).

35. T. S. Eliot, *Little Gidding*.

36. John Feehan, 'Community Development: the Spiritual Dimension.' *Perspectives on Community Development in Ireland* 1(1) (2005), pp 63-74.

37. John Feehan, *A Sense of Place*, Guest Editor Section of *The Local Planet*, Issue 7 (2006), 29-44.

38. John Feehan, 'Finding a heartbeat,' *Trowel*, UCD's Archaeological Student Magazine (2005).

39. See www.rootsweb.ancestry.com/~irlkik/ihm/diocese.htm

40. The Ordnance Survey began the gargantuan task of mapping the townlands of Ireland, all 60,000 of them, in 1825, starting in the north of

the country and working south. The first sheets were published in 1833, and the last in 1846.

41. H.J. Massingham, *The Tree of Life* (1943; new edition Jon Carpenter Publishing, 2003), p 9.

42. Éamon de Valera, Radio broadcast, 17 March 1943.

43. John Feehan, Inaugural World Landscapes Lecture.

44. Jim Collins' recent monograph *Quickening the Earth. Soil Minding and Mending in Ireland* (UCD School of Biology and Environmental Science, 2008) chronicles in detail the thrift and ingenuity with which manures and composts were treasured in an earlier Ireland. Equally remarkable, on a different scale and in an entirely different culture, was the husbanding of the sources of soil fertility in early modern China: see F. H. King, *Farmers of Forty Centuries or Permanent Agriculture in China, Korea and Japan* (1911).

45. Fred Pearce, *The Last Generation*.

46. In spite of the similarity in sound between 'ethic' and 'aesthetic' the two words have entirely different roots, but as we shall see, they metamorphose into each other, at least in the context discussed here. Aesthetic is the Greek *aisthaytikos*: things perceptible by the senses (as distinct from *noaytah*, things that can be thought or imagined).

AFTERWORDS ...

1. James A. Weisheipl, *Friar Thomas D'Aquino: his life, thought and work*, (Washington DC, The Catholic University of America Press, 1983).

2. Huxley, op. cit.

3. Charley D. Hardwick, *Events of grace. Naturalism, existentialism and theology*, CUP, 1996

4. Henry Nelson Wieman, *Religious Experience and Scientific Method*, (Macmillan,1926): 'Whatever else God may mean, it is a term used to designate that Something upon which human life is most dependent for its security, welfare and increasing abundance. The mere fact that human life happens, and continues to happen, proves that this Something, however, unknown, does certainly exist' (pp 9-10).

5. George Tyrrell, *Through Scylla and Charybdis*, p 287.

6. Leonard Hodgson, *On the Authority of the Bible*, (London, SPCK, 1960), p 4. 'There is no such thing as revealed truth. There are truths of revelation, that is to say, propositions which express the result of correct thinking concerning revelation; but they are not themselves directly revealed.' (William Temple, *Nature, Man and God*, p 317).

7. John Feehan, (2005), Review of Sean McDonagh's *The Death of Life*, *The Far East* (July / August), p 16.

8. Vladimir Nabokov, *Speak, Memory: An Autobiography Revisited*, (New York, Putnam, 1966).

9. Jan Swammerdam, *The Book of Nature* (1758), trs Thomas Hill.

Index